THE LEADERSHIP TRIFECTA

Essential Knowledge for the Christian Leader

From the Battlefield–To the Gridiron

JOSEPH WELOCK

ISBN 979-8-88685-792-4 (paperback)
ISBN 979-8-88685-793-1 (digital)

Christian Faith Publishing
832 Park Avenue
Meadville, PA 16335
www.christianfaithpublishing.com

Printed in the United States of America

To Amber, my love, my life, my hero.
I love you with all of my heart.
Thank you, Lord, for placing her in my life.

TABLE OF CONTENTS

For a Warrior to have success—Preparation is the key for mission completion

COMBAT READINESS ESSENTIALS

INDISPENSABLE KNOWLEDGE FOR THE COMBAT EFFECTIVE CHRISTIAN LEADER

BE THE ONE

You may be thinking, what kind of connections can be made when you compare the life and teachings of Jesus Christ, the US Marine Corps, and coaching? Two of the three revolve around violence and hostility, while the other focuses on kindness and compassion. When you first saw this book, you may have been searching for a resource on Jesus's teachings. You may have a love for books about the military. A few of you could have been on the prowl for your next football fix, and this book piqued your interest. Whatever caught your attention, I hope that I am able to help you understand that each of the three above impacted my life in a profound way. I hope that you will take something from this book that allows you to better understand leadership and the importance of bold Christian faith.

When I reflect on the teachings of Jesus Christ, the rich history of the US Marine Corps, and the principles that successful coaches encompass, I have identified many parallels. Most people would agree that for an individual or an organization to succeed, a strong foundation rooted in principles and beliefs are essential. All three incorporate a foundation rooted in sound morals, beliefs, and framework that have been tried and tested to ensure success.

I challenge you to take a few minutes before you read any further and write down a few characteristics or qualities that you identify with Jesus Christ, the Marine Corps, and that of a great coach. I bet that you will be surprised by the similarities that you come up with.

What are Christian values? The following descriptive words pop into my mind: love, fidelity, obedience, commitment, forgiveness, compassion, self-respect, confidence, surrender, honesty, patience, self-control, passion, and respect. These are all words that remind me of my Savior.

When I think of my time in US Marine Corps boot camp, I flash back to my initial training while in Alpha Company Platoon 1082. I instantly sound off with the words honor, courage, devotion, conformity, integrity, sacrifice, faithfulness, dependability, enthusiasm, and unselfishness. In comparison, when I look at what make a great coach, traits like reliability, dedication, truthfulness, tolerance, discipline, expectations, compliance, consistency, and loyalty come to mind.

Now think about the state of our nation in 2021. We live in a society that is crumbling. Look around. There is a blatant lack of respect for authority. There is a major push to keep God out of every part of our lives that some call this secular progressivism. Our government is becoming more and more intrusive every day. Jobs are hard to find and are rapidly becoming outsourced. A lack of jobs is leading to a weaker economic system. When we turn on the television, we hear about the huge decline in the middle class. But the one that scares me the most is that over 50 percent of our marriages end in divorce. Our foundation is coming apart. Our nation is hemorrhaging, and we have to stop the bleeding before it is too late.

It is up to us to place value on and reinstitute the characteristics from the "C3"—Christ, corps, coaching—back into our society. As Christians, we must take the lead. Will you be the one that stands up and fights to save our nation, our children, our future? It can start with one spark. You can be that spark.

A major obstacle that stands out as a football coach is the athlete's intrinsic motivation. A coach must train the athlete to excel beyond his or her own perceived limitations. A coach must consistently motivate the athletes to elevate their level of performance. I constantly tell my coaches that if they are not challenging the athletes physically and mentally, then the athletes are not developing and growing.

I push my athletes to the limit, both mentally and physically. This helps an athlete realize that their capabilities far exceed what their mind and body tell them is possible. Athletes are routinely reminded that they must break out of their comfort level. It is okay to risk and give up some things that some of their friends are doing because the rewards are worth it. It is about investment. Athletes have to understand that their level of investment will dictate their level of success on the playfield.

A strong foundation is essential in athletics and life. From day one, the athletes are told, "*Be the one.*" Be the one that no one is able to outwork. Be the one that no one wants to run the ball toward. Be the man that no one wants to throw the ball toward. Be the man that no one wants to have to cover or try and tackle. Be first in everything that you do, and refuse to be last. Be the example. Be the spark. Why? Because that is what makes you special. When you are the *one*, you are the difference maker.

You may have come across this before:

One in one hundred:

Of every one hundred men, ten shouldn't even be there, eighty are nothing but targets, nine are *real fighters*. We are lucky to have them, for *they make the battle*! But *one*, *one* of them is a *warrior*, and *he* will bring the others back.

This mentality relates to Christian leadership as well as athletics. I challenge you to "be the one." The time is now. We must step out of our complacent and often self-interested ways. There is too much at stake. Our worldly self wants to guide us, but we must not let it. We must place our focus on and set our sight upon our personal walk with the Lord and allow him to show us the path that he needs us to take. We are capable of having a profound impact on those around us. God is with us and will provide the strength and guidance that we need on our journey. I am challenging you to step up and *be the one* for Christ.

Every day I challenge myself to be the strong Christian man that is needed. I get up early and make time to work on my personal relationship with God. Some days I read the Bible, while some days I listen to a sermon on my phone and look to apply and incorporate the teaching into my day. Other days I just pray to God. I thank him for my life and my blessings. I reflect on how unbelievably awesome my life is and ask him to make me a difference maker.

To be clear, as you draw near to Christ, the enemy will take notice. Once you decide to live a Christ-centered life, you will quickly find yourself in the sights of the enemy. At this point, prepare for battle, and strap on the armor of God. The devil stands ready and willing to rage war against you by disrupting your progress and knocking you off your path. The devil will sling arrows at you from every direction. Be prepared for an aggressive attack. Your preparedness is the essential element that will help you defend yourself. The devil is a ferocious and tenacious adversary who wishes only to devour anything that stands in his way. It is imperative that you stay calm and keep your wits about you. Remember that a strong mind and laser-like focus will help you conquer your fears.

Be ready for a "direct action mission." The devil will go on the offensive. To reference and relate this to my experience in the US Marine Corps, a direct action mission is an intensely explosive raid against a target of high value or of great importance. These types of missions are usually of short duration. However, they are extremely explosive with a great amount of emphasis on violence of action. Direct action missions are conducted in order to recover, capture, destroy, or damage a designated target. A predetermined and precise use of force is employed to ensure operational success. Be aware that you will be in a hostile environment as rounds will be fired at you fast and furiously.

It is imperative that we learn to recognize the early signs of an attack. When we identify an attack, call on God for strength because you and I cannot defeat the devil without God's help. It took me a long time to recognize that the war that was raging within and around me was of this manner. Now I understand that success depended on my ability to call in a QRF, or a quick reaction force in military terms, for reinforcement. My greatest asset, God, is there to reinforce me. Today I know the importance of calling on God for support. Jesus Christ has our backs, and he will provide the reinforcements needed to suppress the enemy and rally to victory.

In the Marine Corps, our training incorporated a great deal of rappelling. One of the most intimidating forms of rappel is Australian rappel. Australian rappel is a technique used to descend a fixed rope in a standing position while facing the ground. One major personal obstacle that set many men up to fail on the rappel tower is the internal fear that once you step over the edge, you are going to fall to your death. Australian rappel brought this fear out in the open for many men. One training day, our rappel master made a comment that had profound impact in the moment and has stayed with me my entire life. While on top of a sixty-foot tower, learning to do the Australian rappel, the rappel master smiled at a small group of us and stated, "Don't submit to your fear, just take the leap. That is the hardest part, and it is all downhill from there." He then turned away from us, took his first step, and led the way.

It is time for us to take the leap. Call on God and ask him what his plan is for you. Ask him how he can use you. Have an open mind, and listen for God's advice. Study his word, and apply it to your life. Jesus Christ will not lead you down the wrong path. I listen for his voice. God has a regular conversation with me. He guides me and inspires me daily. I then try and apply what I hear and attack every challenge as if I am *the one*.

ALWAYS FAITHFUL

"Semper fi" is a phrase that I must have heard at least a million times growing up. It seemed to be on every shirt, bumper sticker and was spoken whenever my father's Marine buddies were at the house. As a young boy, I was taught that the phrase "Semper fi" is used as a way to verbally identify with someone who is a part of a brotherhood. Semper fidelis is deeply rooted in Marine Corps history, and it is a way of life for all Marines. Semper fidelis is much more than a silly slogan. Marines are not sometimes faithful, rather they are always faithful. The motto is nonnegotiable, an absolute. "Semper fi" means and demands something to those who utter it, causing Marines to swell with pride when they use this transgenerational phrase.

My childhood development was rooted in the Marine Corps ethos, values, and beliefs. My father was a twenty-eight-year veteran who demanded only the best from my brother and I. Today, when I reflect back on that period of my life, I will admit that many of the lessons learned were not enjoyable, teachable moments. I will admit that I gained valuable knowledge from and am stronger mentally due to these experiences. I must say that my father played an instrumental part in setting the foundation for the man that I am today.

As a boy, I was taught devotion and dedication. It was explained to me that it was my duty, as both an American and as a Welock, to join the Marine Corps. My father was preparing the next generation of devil dog. As a Welock, you quickly grasped an understanding for the meaning of "instant obedience to orders." So becoming a Marine was a way of solidifying the transformation from boy to man. After eighteen years of growing up immersed in Marine Corps tradition, graduating from Marine Corps boot camp was one of the greatest days of my life.

Earning the title of Marine was expected and demanded. I knew no other path than following the Marine Corps path and becoming a warrior. Shortly after high school graduation, I headed straight to boot camp. My boot camp platoon, platoon 1082, started with seventy-plus recruits and graduated less than forty. After thirteen weeks of hell, I was marching across the MCRD parade deck in my dress blues, filled with an unbelievable amount of personal pride and feeling of accomplishment. I remember thinking I had accomplished the mission. I had finally become a full-fledged member of the brotherhood. I had achieved something that I had mentally been prepared for and had poured my blood, sweat, and tears into. I have earned the title and become a member of an elite few.

As a Welock male, I was to become a warrior and dedicate myself to the mission of defending my great nation through unselfish devotion to something that was greater than myself. This engrained mindset helped me integrate into the Marine Corps. As a Marine, I was to live by the core values of honor, courage, and commitment. My duty would be to protect the legacy of and carry on the heritage of those that came before me.

The Marine Corps does not place value on individuality. Rather, the Marine Corps places high value on unit cohesiveness. It promotes teamwork, along with loyalty to the brotherhood, all of which is vital for unit success. I constantly find myself reflecting on this important aspect and relate it to my walk with God. Even though I fail God on a daily basis, he is always faithful.

In the morning, in my personal time with God, I ask him for guidance and direction. I listen and open my heart and mind for what he is trying to tell me. It is amazing how often I am reminded that I must live by a code. As Christians, we are taught to act Christlike and set the example for others to follow. Christians must be men and women of integrity. It is our duty to be distinctly different than and stand out from others. Christians must embrace the highest ethics, standards, and morality. It is our duty to set the example. It is our responsibility to lead the way. This is something that I can easily relate to due to my Marine Corps training. Due to parallels between Christianity and the Marine Corps, I regularly compare the Marine Corps core values of honor, courage, and commitment and integrate the two philosophies within my life.

As a Christian leader, you have to be courageous. Be bold, step out, and conquer your fear. Tough decisions will have to be made every day. One of the most difficult struggles will be consistent decision making. Wake up every day with a plan of attack. Focus on your objective, and keep your mind on your goal, providing an example of consistent Christian leadership.

I have observed and identified a lack of consistency in our society; but unfortunately, there is also a lack of consistency in the modern church. Our society places emphasis on the church's lack of consistent hypocrisy. Sadly, Christians are often seen as hypocrites. The lack of consistency that many Christians represent has tainted society's view of the church. It is time for this to change. It is up to us to be courageous. But courage is not enough. Consistency is key, but the hypocrisy has to go. God is consistently faithful to us, and now is the time for us to be consistently faithful in return. It is time to elevate our level of commitment and change our society's view and opinion of American Christ followers.

As a Marine, when faced with an ambush, we are taught to attack the enemy. Training dictates that we are to overcome the enemy by quickly obtaining *fire superiority* over the enemy and counter attack through fire and maneuver. As Christian role models, we must stand up for right and wrong. In the hard times, when others surrender in the heat of the battle, it is our responsibility to attack the enemy to lead the charge. We must have the determination of mind that allows us to stay the course and complete the mission. As Christian leaders, we must decisively and effectively stand up to face down the enemy and refuse to accept defeat. The stakes are too high.

What is at stake, you ask? The lives and families of the children we have today. Our personal legacy hangs on the decisions we make every day. But more importantly, the number of souls in heaven depends on how we live our lives and the example that we set. To put it in military terms, it is time to stand in the gap. We must be the ones who rise up and run toward the sound of gunfire. As Christian leaders, we must be the tip of the spear. We must be prepared and poised to react and respond when we identify a spiritual assault. No matter what mission we are tasked with, we must be the few, the proud, the elite warrior that will fearlessly sprint toward the chaos.

DREAMS AND REALITY

As a child, we all dream. At a young age, many children dream of being firemen, policemen, nurses, or doctors. We buy toys related to these jobs and even wear clothes or costumes and play games with our friends where we act as if we were actively doing these jobs. But eventually, we all grow up and move past playing games. By the time we reach high-school age, a good number of us decide on a career that we believe is our ideal job. After high school, some of us have the motivation and economic ability to reach these goals, while others find themselves in a situation where they struggle to achieve them. Sadly, there are a good number of young people who make the individual choice to not attack their goals and do not study or push themselves and find success. In doing so, perceived dreams are crushed before they are achieved.

At a young age, we recognize that time is precious, and each of us decides how to prioritize our time. Once we reach high school, we craft a plan that will get us to graduation. Many take high school seriously, while others blow off classes. In doing so, we ultimately set the tone for our lives. During these developmental years, sadly, many of us do not understand the importance of the lessons learned behind the teacher's instruction. Too often we place more focus on the time spent on schoolwork as wasted time that it takes away from what we perceive as important—i.e., sports, part-time job, video games. If only we had appreciated the value gained through our participation in the educational process. Sadly, we do not have the wisdom to understand that we are carving out our future path, and our journey's success is achieved by today's hard work.

Sometimes we are not able to identify obstacles that are in our path, just as a hurdler will run into hurdles if he only focuses on the finish line. We have to recognize that there are tasks in the process that, through accomplishment, allow us to turn our dreams into a reality.

It is not the end of the world when a dream does not come true. God provides these experiences to provide lessons that will help guide us in our decision-making later in life. It is amazing that God will allow us to go through specific obstacles that we may see as world ending, but in reality, they are only game changing. God will allow us to fail so that we obtain knowledge that can help us later. I will admit, it took me a long time to understand one important concept that good and bad life experiences, the trials, and tribulations of our lives are all placed there for a purpose.

I believe that God has a specific path and goal in mind for each of us. God has given us free will and has a plan for each of us. Our specific life experiences provide useful knowledge and wisdom that can help us at a later time. It is how we use this knowledge and wisdom that is important. I now understand that each and every one of my life experiences have taken place for a reason and not simply by chance.

> Blessed is the one who perseveres under trial because, having stood the test, that person will receive the crown of life that the Lord has promised to those who love him. (James 1:12)

Early in my coaching career, I often wondered why certain people had opportunities presented to them while I seemed to never be in the right place at the right time. I was focused on climbing the coaching ladder. I applied for coaching positions that I was not seen as prepared for or had the right connection for. Then one day, I prayed to God, and rather than ask for a specific job, I asked him to place me where he needed me. I trusted my career to him and no longer chased titles or positions. I would leave the advancement of my position in his hands. The Lord had a plan for my life. I focused on doing the best job that I could where I was at. My focus was redirected on impacting as many people as I am able within my circle of influence.

I had come to the realization that my experiences, successes, dreams, and perceived failures may or may not necessarily be for my own personal gain. Rather, all that I had or had not accomplished may have taken place not for my own gain but so others could learn or grow from the experiences that had taken place. My life choices may potentially cause someone to recognize they have a need for God in their life.

For the longest time, I thought about successes and failures and only related them to myself. I had a selfish, self-centered mindset when it came to results. I was not egotistical but rather focused on only the individual reward. I did not understand that a positive or a negative that surrounded a situational event may not be fully seen or understood for years to come. A current result or outcome in an event may play into a future circumstance that may potentially have zero relation to my own life. What it really comes down to is this: "And we know that in all things God works for the good of those who love him, who have been called according to his purpose" (Romans 8:28). I have come to a place in my life where I believe God knew what was best for me because He lights my path and places me where he needed me.

My success as a coach and the legacy that I leave is not based on wins and losses in athletics. I now know that I am blessed with a family who love me, and I feel comfort in knowing that my true legacy, my children, will spend eternity in heaven with my wife and me. Every choice that I have made or experience in my life has taken place to prepare me for the present and future. I am human, and I make mistakes. I reflect on and learn from the positives and negatives in my life. I know that God is there for me and that he will strengthening me, guide me, and never abandon me. I trust in him, and I thank him for his sacrifice.

> For the wages of sin is death, but the gift of God
> is eternal life in Christ Jesus our Lord. (Romans
> 6:23)

God has promised us that the battles we face and the tough times in life are all there for a reason. I constantly remind athletes of a sign above our drill instructor's office in Marine Corps boot camp. "That which does not kill us only makes us stronger." I was part of an outstanding football program in high school and was pushed physically. But in Marine Corps boot camp, I experienced a new level of pain. In boot camp, one is physically and mentally pushed to his/her limits. Many recruits are thrashed unmercifully on the quarterdeck of the squad bay. By enduring the physical hell that your body has to endure for extended periods of time, recruits recognize that his/her mind is able to achieve much more than perceived. Our struggles have a purpose; and by battling through each obstacle, we obtain a reward and add strength that we can fall back on when tough times hit us in the future.

Satan battles to ultimately take away all that we have been given and have been blessed with. I find my strength in Jesus and know that he is my rock. Jesus is my provider, my comforter. Thank you, Jesus, for providing me the focus and guidance to be victorious, not only in physical battle but when the mental battle rages.

> The LORD is a warrior; the LORD is his name.
> (Exodus 15:3)

FRAG ORDER

A "Frag order" is an abbreviated operation order. In the military, it is commonly issued day-to-day and is set up to eliminate the need for restating information contained in a basic operation order that takes place over a period of days/weeks. Flexibility is essential in a hostile environment. Frag orders are often necessary due to enemy movements or when changing tactics that are employed. We must expect that every plan will change. No plan survives upon initial contact with the enemy, and flexibility is a key to success.

I am a Christian. I am a husband to a wonderful woman and have been blessed with two beautiful and spirited daughters. I am a US Marine, a warrior, a leader, and a graduate of the University of Texas at Austin. I am an educator. As a high school football coach, I have been entrusted with the responsibility and opportunity to develop today's boys into tomorrow's leaders. I live a life that I can be proud of. Overall, I am most thankful that God has provided me a journey in my forty-plus years on this planet where I have encountered both highs and lows. I am the person I am today because of lessons learned throughout my life experiences and the choices that I have made during my journey. I attribute my success to the solid foundation instilled while in the Marine Corps and the guidance of a God who is steadfast and faithful.

I believe that the stronger you are, the more impact that you are capable of having, and the harder the devil attacks you. I will be the first to tell you that I have made many poor choices, and the devil knows where I am the weakest. On a daily basis, the enemy bombards me. He is attempting to derail me and disrupt my walk with the Lord. The enemy constantly entices me to walk a path that will distance me from God. But that is where training and God's guidance comes into play.

I have a background in intelligence gathering. If it were not for my ability to gather intel, I would not understand my opponent's strategy, nor would I be able to identify the tactics that he employs. The devil is well versed in the art of war. He is quick to change his point of attack and will incorporate a flanking maneuver when I least expect it. I am a warrior. I am able to identify the signs of an oncoming conflict.

> Even though I walk through the darkest valley, I
> will fear no evil, for you are with me; your rod
> and your staff, they comfort me. (Psalm 23:4)

Just as it is the Marine Corps motto, "SEMPER FI" is also Jesus's motto.

> The LORD himself goes before you and will be
> with you; he will never leave you nor forsake
> you. Do not be afraid; do not be discouraged.
> (Deuteronomy 31:8)

I found Jesus while I was in middle school, but my time with Christ was short-lived. I was a spirited young man who was easily distracted. Due to circumstances, situations, experiences, and choices in life, I quickly turned away from God. By the time I graduated from high school, I was no longer focused on God or attending church. I spent the next eighteen years living life by my own rules and the direction that I wanted to go. It was not until 2010 that I finally decided it was time to follow my spiritual compass. It was time to make some, and I strove to live my life and follow "the will of my Father in heaven."

From the moment I started to make changes in my life, I became a target. The devil did not want to release his hold on me. Still there is not a day that goes by that the enemy does not confront me. The devil is a persistent foe; therefore, I have to call on God for daily support. I have come to realize that the more I immerse myself in and study God's word, the stronger I feel. I am a believer that God does draw closer to me as long as I draw close to him. He provides me the strength to fight my personal battles and to ultimately conquer my personal demons.

The enemy shells me every day. The devil likes to drop bombs on me. He constantly employs method after method of attack in hopes of derailing my trek. Just as a Marine on the battlefield has to understand the tactics of his opponent or a football coach has to be able to identify the tactics when he is relentlessly blitzed by the defense to disrupt the timing of the offense. It is imperative that I stay the course, keep my vision on the mission, and overcome the obstacles and adversities that are placed in my path, whether large or small.

I met my wife in high school. One December evening, I decided to drive up to our high school and watch our basketball team play our crosstown rival. I walked, sat in the stands, surveyed the crowd, and saw the most beautiful cheerleader I had ever laid my eyes upon. I was starstruck. I went home that night and told my mom that I had just seen the woman I was going to marry. The first time I saw Amber Taylor Welock, I knew it was love at first sight. I literally had been struck by cupid's arrow.

The sad part was, I quickly learned that her family would be moving to New Jersey in only a few months. I fell deeply in love with Amber. We spent a decent amount of time together in the evenings. I would drive over to her house and hang out with her and her family. I felt feelings toward Amber that I had never felt toward anyone I had ever met. I can honestly say that, for the first time in my life, I fell in love, which led to my first heartbreak. Amber and I were both in different places in our lives and going in opposite directions, with very little time to get to know each other. Once Amber left Texas, our relationship ended, and shortly thereafter, so did our friendship. I was devastated. But today I understand how everything that takes place in our lives happens for a reason, and I thank God every day that he placed her back in my life. Today, Amber is my rock, my best friend, my foundation, and my hero.

A little background on me: I was brought up in the Southern Baptist Church and have read the Bible in depth. As previously stated, I accepted Jesus as my Savior in middle school. My family attended church regularly, but my homelife was atrocious. Strict military discipline, fighting, abuse, and negativity were the norm. We went to church regularly and looked the part. But behind closed doors, reality was very different.

Upon finishing high school, I made the decision that living in an atmosphere where my focus seemed to be placed on tiptoeing around abusive behavior that involved constant fighting and negativity was not the place for me. I wanted a fresh start, and I made a plan to get out of Mesquite, Texas. All I wanted was an opportunity to grow and experience life in a new place. So I did what I was trained to do, and I joined the US Marine Corps. I hopped the first plane out of town that the recruiter could get me on and headed to Marine Corp Recruit Depot San Diego.

I was welcomed with open arms as I took my first steps off the plane. I was welcomed by a Marine drill instructor standing in the airport, instructing us what needed to be done in order for us to begin the process that lay ahead of us. While at MCRD, I was the recipients of excellent training, structure, discipline, and horrible food. The Marine Corps is known for its ability to mold average teenagers into exceptional Americans. I became a member of a brotherhood. I felt comfort knowing that I had surrounded myself with men who had been through the same crucible of training. The Marine Corps had a major impact on my life because I was forged into a warrior.

As a Marine, I met many great men from all over the world. I experienced many new places and interacted with new people and cultures. Some of my best friends and greatest memories come from my time in the Marine Corps. Depending on one's job specialty, he/she may be presented with the opportunity to attend many combat training courses that revolve around urban combat training and jungle warfare training. Many infantry Marines end up with a great deal of counterterrorism training, advanced marksmanship and ultimately become skilled in close-quarter battles.

Together we learned to overcome trials and tribulations. We understood how important it was to have someone you can depend on no matter how difficult the situation may be. As infantry Marines, we pushed each other and competed against each other in everything that we did. We knew each other's strengths and weaknesses and sacrificed for each other. Ultimately, we became men.

But the Marine Corps is not all roses and teddy bears. You will eventually find yourself in a compromising position or location. I was an example of the prototypical US Marine. I lived, breathed, and slept the warrior mindset. Great focus was put on being the best Marine that I could be, but I was a horrible man. I lived life to the fullest. I observed and experienced some of the worst things one could imagine while in the Marines. I think, it is safe to say, I ultimately got as far away from God as one could get. I was angry. It was easy for me to be and stay angry as a Marine. As an infantry Marine, your job revolves around aggressive action. This fed my ego, actions, and mental state. We ultimately epitomized the saying "work hard, play harder."

The one thing that a platoon full of angry Marines knows what to do is drink. I fueled myself with the warriors' brew—alcohol. The combination of anger and alcohol led to a great deal of depression. There are many Marines that would consistently drink with me under the table, but I have blown many paychecks in two- to three-day time period. If you did not know, alcohol and infantry are synonymous.

Sadly, alcohol and depression are also synonymous. Depression is something that I have struggled with for a large portion of my life. Depression and the Marine Corps go hand in hand just as ammunition and weapons go together. It has only been the last six to seven years that I truly understood the impact that depression had on my life.

As a young Marine, I was still struggling with a lot of things from my early life experiences. I placed a lot of blame on and became angry with God and at one point felt hate toward him. I questioned the fact that God was all-powerful. I could not believe that he would allow certain things to happen in this world. I was eaten up with anger. If this really was a world that he had complete power over, why did he allow rape, murder, death, and destruction to take place? In response to these feelings, I turned my back on God.

Today, I am thankful that God never turned his back on me. I do not deserve nor am I worthy of God's forgiveness, but he never gave up on me. His actions are a perfect example of covenant. God never abandoned me, yet He protected me in times of danger, literally saving my life on more than one occasion.

As stated, I am unworthy of forgiveness. God's forgiveness provision is readily identifiable throughout my life. The second most powerful example of this was when Amber Taylor walked back into my life. Amber heard word that my father had passed away, and she reached out to me while I was stationed in California. We were on opposite sides of our continent, taking different paths, but something made her call me. I believe today that God had it in his plan and nudged her to do so. Amber made that call more out of a sense of obligation due to her Southern upbringing than out of true mercy.

Amber's upbringing was almost the polar opposite of mine. Amber's parents have been married for more than forty years. John and Dianna are still completely in love and have rarely fought in front of their children or in front of me. Amber was raised in the church, but she has stated to me that her focus was more on the people than the purpose. When her family moved to New Jersey at the age of fourteen, they became unchurched, not knowing how to fit in a community that was predominantly Jewish and Catholic.

We slowly rebuilt our relationship by initially becoming friends. This friendship grew, and I remember the very deep and real pain of being apart from her. Since this was during the pre-/early cell phone era, I would call Amber on the pay phone in our barracks as often as I could. I eventually racked up a consistent four-hundred-dollar-a-month AT&T calling card bill. I was drawing close to her as a person. I was amazed and in awe of the true woman that she was.

Amber's feeling for me grew as well. On one occasion, Amber told me that I made her feel safe, that I made her feel beautiful, and that I made her feel as if she could do anything. I was amazed that I could have this type of impact on such an amazing person. We both fell in love, and I could not wait to spend the rest of my life with this young lady. Though months and a few years went by, we both thought that we would never take each for granted once we were together because we already knew how hard it was to be apart. Boy, were we ever wrong in our naive thoughts.

As with any military enlistment contract, eventually time runs out, and a choice must be made. Marines must either sign another contract or transition to the civilian world. I loved being a Marine, but I knew that if I wanted to have a life that included Amber, I would have to forge a new path. So instead of reenlisting, I decided to move to Austin, Texas, and work toward obtaining a college degree at the University of Texas at Austin.

I Amber and I moved into a seven-hundred-square-foot apartment together. Things went well for a while, but eventually the newness wore off. A small apartment, pressure to do well in college, and both of us working full-time jobs added an extra level of pressure to the equation. First there were fights about our roles in the household, and then there were fights about money. We had a fair share of nasty fights that ended up with both of us crying in each other's arms. Amber and I were both young and stubborn, but we managed to push through the obstacles as they presented themselves.

I graduated from the University of Texas the same time that Amber finished UT law school. Once we moved to Dallas and settled into our real jobs, the fights became even more frequent due to both having work schedules that stretched us thin. Our time together was not quality time, yet it became an opportunity to vent frustration and time to argue. Once again, we pushed through, and our relationship seemed to level off.

After just one year renting an old condo in Dallas, Amber and I decided to purchase our first home. We thought that buying a house was the next step in building a strong relationship. It is funny how we make choices in life. We both believed that this purchase would help us bond. Our hope was that all of the small decisions that we would have to make together, like picking furniture and decorations, would bring Amber and me closer. Looking back, the added economic weight of the house purchase and all the small purchases that go along with it only added to our stress level.

It was not until we decided to have children that we ultimately realized how busy life can be. Amber and I are unbelievably blessed with two wonderful girls, but we quickly realized that before children, we had no clue how stressful family life could be. We lived life on a roller coaster. But the addition of children to the equation took our stress to a whole new level. Our relationship would have periods of really good times and periods of really bad times.

After the birth of our second daughter, many people believed that we had the perfect little family and were living the American dream. We had great jobs and were very successful. Everything that we had, we worked for and purchased ourselves. We had college degrees, careers, children, a nice house, and a decent amount of money. What others could not see was we were a broken and frustrated duo who individually felt as if we had lost our way.

Our relationship paralleled my childhood experience but with a far lesser degree of anger and frustration. Amber and I eventually lost respect for each other. After twenty-two years of marriage, we knew exactly what to say to hurt the other. We stayed up night after night fighting and lost countless hours of sleep arguing about who could get the last word.

Amber and I fought all the time. We became focused more on who would win the argument than clearing up the situation. Maybe it was a way of relieving ourselves of the angst that we were feeling. Amber and I both cried buckets of tears. It felt as if we were right back to the same position that we were in while living in our small seven-hundred-square-foot apartment in Austin, Texas. It became apparent to our family and friends that something was wrong, and we were both to blame.

The fighting continued, but eventually the tears stopped. One night, during an argument, we both came to the realization that we didn't feel as if we cared about each about each other anymore. We spoke cavalierly about divorce, but neither of us could stand the idea of not being with the children every single day. We both hoped that the love of and for our children would be enough to make us happy, but it seemed like divorce was the only option that we had left. We were most definitely standing at the crossroads.

In part, due to my childhood experiences, all I had ever known in a husband-wife relationship was fighting. I was tired and fed up with feeling pain and wanted the pain and frustration to stop. We did not respect each other, and I missed love down deep that neither of us wanted our relationship to end. I loved my wife and children, and I wanted our marriage to be better, and I wanted our family to be better. I prayed that our relationship would get back to where we were when we were young and in love. The funny thing was I had literally no relationship with God at this time and was just looking for hope.

Amber and I both understood how blessed we were in our lives. I thought maybe I had been going about this all the wrong way. Maybe I needed to fall back on my roots. Maybe God was the answer that I was looking for. Despite my personal wrestling match that I had had with God over the years, I figured that I would swallow my pride and start attending a local church because I felt convicted deep inside. I thought that if anything could bring us together, God could save our marriage.

I knew we needed an outside source of strength, compassion, devotion, honesty, and forgiveness to draw from and lean on. Consequently, I began researching possible churches to attend nearby. I spoke to a neighbor and picked the brains of a few coworkers who attend another nearby church in hopes of finding a church that would be our first test-drive.

I emailed the pastor at Elevate Church in Murphy, Texas, and interviewed him on his church's core beliefs. I looked into Elevate due to the fact that it had been an old feedstore. I was initially drawn to Elevate because of my familiarity of the building and loved the fact that Elevate Church has a history of being a barn, a source of sustenance and refuge.

I had questions that I needed answered. I was blunt with Pastor Kalyn Brassfield. I spoke with him about some of my beliefs and questioned him about the fundamental values and attitudes of Elevate Church. I believed that Jesus had died for my sins. I had chosen the spiritual path that I was currently on and understood that it was partially to blame for my current situation. However, I needed to feel out the church before I walked in the doors. After several emails over a couple of weeks, I finally told Amber that I wanted to take the family and visit Elevate Church.

The first time I entered Elevate, I was a bit thrown by how different this church felt. It was set up and flowed differently than the church I grew up in. I had a Southern Baptist upbringing and quickly realized that Elevate church was different. What happened next shocked both Amber and I. The very first week we were there, Kalyn spoke about how to be a better parent. He read a passage from a book *Bringing Up Girls* that applied just as much to my young daughters as it did to my wife. Amber and I both wept openly. I felt drained but also empowered. After church, we went to lunch as a family and talked about our experience at Elevate as a family. Each one of us felt empowered. Our spirits were high, and our bond felt stronger. We had a great lunch and spent quality, stress-free time together.

The girls loved their morning at Elevate and spoke about God and Jesus as if they had just discovered a secret! After lunch, we went and bought bikes for both my wife and I so that we could spend more quality time as a family. We ended the afternoon going on a family bike ride and getting caught in the rain. Three of us were laughing hysterically, while the youngest of our family, Landry, screamed at the top of her lungs as she pedaled her tail off with the biggest smile I had ever seen on her face. Landry's behavior in particular made for an awesome memory and a great day.

This was truly a day like never before for our family. In fact, it was the first of many. The very next week, Pastor Kalyn spoke about how to be a better partner. Again, Amber and I both cried crocodile tears in church. We both began reading the Bible on a regular basis. I used to jokingly say that Amber knew everything so long as it was in a book. She was a brilliant woman that seemed to have no common sense. But we had virtually ignored the only book that really mattered.

After attending Elevate for a few weeks, our marital relationship began to strengthen. On a higher note, we began to build a relationship with God. We quit talking about "the" God and began to speak of "my" God. Not to mention, our kids started singing worship songs as they played in the house. Overall, life seemed to be moving in a much better direction.

Just as we had so many years before, we started to rebuild our relationship. Putting the hurt behind us, Amber and I were kind to each other again and realized that we enjoyed spending quality time together. Then we came under attack. Amber and I started to bicker one night. I could feel the tension starting to rise and knew that this might not be going in the right direction. I abruptly stopped, sat down on the couch next to Amber, and asked her to pray with me. It was the first time that we had ever done this. Slowly the ever-present tension that filled every corner of our house seemed to disappear. This moment helped me realize that this family was absolutely something worth fighting for, and I was so thankful for this realization.

Let me make it clear, our story has not ended like a fairy tale. We are not perfect, and we still have an occasional fight. I struggle every day with the devil because of the constant attack by evil forces. The devil is my enemy, and I battle with him daily. Just as God knows what to say to me, so does the devil. I have learned, when I feel the "dark side" creeping up on me, I am able to lean on God for strength. The best part is Jesus helps me through each and every struggle. He protects and provides in my time of need. Ultimately, Amber and I both realize that we are not in this battle alone. When we identify an attack, we turn to God for strength.

Jesus's example of steadfast devotion is the reason Amber and I have rededicated our lives to each other. With his guidance, I believe there is nothing that the enemy can do to break us apart. I have complete faith in God. Ultimately, we understand that today our problems are less about Joe versus Amber but more about the struggle between good versus evil.

One verse that continues to speak to us both on this issue is found in Luke 19:41–44.

These verses explain that "as Jesus approached Jerusalem and saw the city, he wept over it and said, 'If you, even you, had only known on this day what would bring you peace—but it's hidden from your eyes. The days will come upon you when your enemies will build an embankment against you and encircle you and hem you in on every side. They will dash you to the ground, you and the children within your walls. They will not leave one stone on another, because you didn't recognize the time of God's coming to you."

These verses also state that not only will we be brought down but so will our children. Just as Jesus wept over Jerusalem, I believe he weeps over troubled marriages and families. God's grace can bring peace and love into everyday lives and into marriages. The enemies that are described within these verses could also be compared to the things that Amber and I allowed to come between us as a couple. We were no longer living in a loving covenant.

Our family spent a good deal of time at Elevate the next three to four months. We were soaking in everything that we could and becoming a part of the church family. Amber and I were approached by a church leadership and asked to tell our story. Amber and I both agreed that we should share our story. We are able to relate to families out there that are currently on the brink, at the crossroads. The devil is driven to tear families apart and knows that the best way to destroy our legacy is to destroy our marriages. He desperately wants our children. And what better way to reach our children than to rip apart the stability that surrounds them.

As Christian leaders, we must strive to be the positive example and provide godly guidance for our children. But we are not able to do this if we are poor husbands and wives. We must be the example that society should look to. We cannot give lip service because our society is at the crossroads. Sometimes people are the problem that is standing in the way of God's blessings. These moments may provide us the opportunity to open the door to God. I pray that I am a tool, used by God, to provide wisdom for those in need. Imagine if God could use you to steer someone in the proper direction.

SELFLESS LOVE

There has to be mutual respect, devotion and a mutual agreement between man and woman if you want a lasting relationship. This is paramount if you plan to raise godly children. Christian leadership must start in the home. A strong relationship must be centered on selfless love. A strong Christian leader must put time and effort into growing this leadership characteristic within themselves and for those that they are able to immediately impact. Strong, selfless leaders should naturally place major emphasis on their loved ones' needs and desires before and above their own wants.

As a teacher, coach, and husband, I come in contact with many people on a daily basis. I have the ability to see people in from multiple generations and interact with them on multiple levels and various platforms. One thing that stands out to me is the lack of unconditional, sacrificial love in our society today.

This mentality starts at the foundation of the family. It is responsibility of the husband and wife to set an example and provide the guidance that our children need. Unfortunately, I see parents spending very little personal time with their children. Most of the time, men in particular are not involved in their daughter's activities. Maybe this is due to the macho persona that society engrains in us, but I believe men act selfishly when they refuse to go to events or spend time doing things that are of great interest to their children. A lack of devotion to your spouse and children has caused splintered relationships throughout our nation.

As a coach, I have noticed an ever-increasing focus on *me* instead of us in the athletic realm. Many contribute or place blame for the state of our culture on the economy, our current administration, what kids watch on TV, or the video games that parents allow their children to play. Personally, I believe those are just excuses. I will be brutally honest with you and tell you that the cultural decay of our society stems from a lazy, self-centered generation of parents.

We are plugged in. Each and every one of us has instant access to things that past generations could not imagine. Any question can be answered with a quick search on our phone or portable electronic device. I believe that the American society is focused on personal comfort, which has been the downfall of many historical world powers. I fear that we will be the next world power to succumb to this failure.

Parents have placed the responsibility of raising children on the back burner. Instead of selfless love, mankind has become enamored with self-love. We allow our children to sit in rooms and play video games for hours or explore the Internet on personal electronic devices while we focus on ourselves. The electronic device has become the new babysitter. It is scary that people allow their children the use of uncensored electronics and grant access to these devices for unlimited amounts of time. Our current culture is struggling with personal responsibility. Why? Because Americans are only focused on "me."

As a coach, I am pulled to this Bible verse: "Watch your life and doctrine closely. Persevere in them, because if you do, you will save both yourself and your hearers" (1 Timothy 4:16). When I decided to become a coach, I became a role model for hundreds and eventually thousands of young men and women. I understood and accepted that it is as much my role and duty to raise up strong young men and women of character as it is to develop them as athletes. I place a major emphasis on the character and leadership development of the athletes that are entrusted to me. But why are there not red flags popping up everywhere when society accepts that it is the responsibility of our teachers and coaches to raise our children? Sadly, it seems as if today's parents are satisfied with what teachers and TV are giving our children in the form of ethics, morals, and beliefs.

It is the duty and responsibility of the parent to raise his/her children with sound ethics, morals and beliefs. But how often do you hear blame being placed on the teacher or the educational system when students fail or make poor choices? We are more than happy to place the blame on someone or something else when our selfishness leads to our children's failure. A strong foundation has to be set at home. Our children are our most precious blessing, and we are content with someone else filling the gap as we go off and focus on our own selfish desires.

In every locker room across the nation or any business meeting that takes place, we hear the words sacrifice, unselfishness, integrity, and loyalty. How can we constantly speak these words over and over, but many people do not model them in their daily lives? There are many people who talk the talk but refuse to walk the walk, and the problem spans all aspects of our society. I have seen it in the military, as a teacher, and as a coach. I pride myself on consistency and expect that those around me understand that others are always watching and judging.

As a child, I experienced inconsistent behavior firsthand. We went to church every Sunday; my father and mother played the perfect roles to represent a model family. Behind closed doors, I saw a different side. I lived in a dysfunctional home that was vastly different from what those on the outside saw. If I were to pick an animal to represent my father, I would have to choose the Tasmanian devil; his temperament and actions were similar. When we returned home from work, it was as if a whirlwind of aggression, violence, and abusiveness blew through the house. I eventually came to the point where I did not want my father at home at all. I learned from this experience and applied the lessons learned and made a promise to myself that I would not continue this cycle. I would create a loving, nurturing environment for my children to grow up.

As Christians, I am challenging you to pick up the torch and be the light. Be the influence that America needs. This task is not easy. You will hit road bumps as do I. The devil will place obstacles along the way to disrupt your path to success. You will get stuck in mud and make bad decisions, but it is vital for the spiritual health of our families and our culture that both the husband and the wife equally sacrifice and show unselfish devotion to each other and to their children. In doing so, we provide visual example and have the potential to influence those around us in a positive fashion.

To reiterate what I stated before, the biggest roadblock in relationships is selfishness. This usually stems from a lack of personal maturity and discipline but ultimately a lack of spiritual maturity and focus on priorities. In other words, we are not wise enough to understand the impact that we are having when we make the choices that we do. Adults have to stop the selfish behavior if we hope to shape those in our circle of influence in a positive way.

Selfless love must start in our homes. We are not able to provide the love and support to our children if we are all caught up in our own ego, selfishness, and pride. Men, the Bible states that you are the spiritual leader of the home. Be exactly that.

> But I want you to realize that the head of every man
> is Christ, and the head of the woman is man, and
> the head of Christ is God. (1 Corinthians 11:3)

Ladies, I know this verse can easily rub a woman the wrong way. This is a touchy subject to many people. I ask you to take a deep breath and keep reading. Amber makes a more substantial amount of money than I do. If you look at success in relation to monetary aspects only, Amber is by far my superior. From a worldly perspective, as an educator/coach, I am the weak link in our relationship.

Try not to look at the male/female roles in a worldly fashion. It is written in the Bible that women are to support their husband. Let me put my touch on this and hopefully clear this up a little for some of you who have ego/gender issues, both male and female. Woman was placed on this planet to complete man. Men have weakness and have the potential to be selfish. Woman strengthens the man in places that he is lacking and in need of support. My wife is the glue that keeps my family together. She is often providing levelheaded input that I need when dealing with difficult or stressful situations. Amber is my number one gift from God. Without her, I would not be the man that I am today. Amber is an amazing woman. I look up to her. I thank God every day for placing her in my life.

Women, please understand that you are as important, as influential, and as needed in comparison to any man on this planet. Men, know that you are not superior to women. They are our equals. My wife is my best friend. She is my strength, my rock, the one that has always been and will always be there to help guide and direct me when times are tough. Amber completes me. A man should allow his wife to do her job, provide the opportunity and support that she needs to be the strong influence that she can be. She is as capable and as powerful as you are. Women are our teammates in the game of life and should be treated as an equal.

Women were made for this role, and God made her to be an ally for the man. Working side by side, success comes from both persons equally taking on their responsibility to overcome the obstacles that present themselves in our lives. This allegiance, devotion, and unselfish dependability are the keys to victory over the enemy who wants to tear our families and culture apart.

Women, as coleaders of the family, should not sit back and allow men to neglect this responsibility. My wife makes a point to ensure that I am fulfilling my role. I do not look at my wife with discontent or frustration when she corrects me or redirects my actions. Instead, I appreciate her effort. I know that she is doing her job and filling the gap. Amber is doing the job that God placed her on this planet to do.

Amber Welock will quickly call me out and let me know if I am slipping in my duties or attitude. Just the other day, our family was sitting on the couch after a long day of work and attending my girl's cheerleading practice. My youngest daughter was throwing an all-out fit in the middle of the room. She was acting in such a manner because she was completely drained physically and mentally. I was not handling a stressful situation with my daughter as I should. I had lost my patience. Amber quickly looked me in the eyes and said, "Someone has gotten a hold of you tonight, hasn't he?" Instinctively I wanted to confront Amber about the comment, but my considerate, perceptive side quickly understood what she was saying. Instead of lashing out at my youngest, I reflected inwardly and made sure to respond appropriately to the situation.

Women, if your husband is not strong enough or capable enough to fulfill his responsibility as the spiritual leader, then it is up to you to take the lead. Men, it is at this point when you need to take notes and let the lesson soak in that you are not fulfilling your duty. There will be times when husbands and wives have to depend on each other to pick up the torch and lead the way. We must honor and serve our family with sacrificial love. Love acts. It demonstrates. Leadership is serving, praising, guiding, and correcting. To be a Christ-filled man or woman, we have to give up our sense of self and our conceit. We must put our time into what is most important—our loved ones. Ultimately, our children are our legacy.

A SHAPED CHARGE!

shaped charge is an explosive charge that has been formed in such a way as to focus the effect of the explosive's energy into an object. When I look at leadership, I think of a shaped charge. Each of us has the ability to have an explosive and lasting effect on the world. I believe God has placed each of us in the current position that we are in today to fulfill a specific job. Our energy, like an exploding shaped charge, if shaped, positioned, and used properly, can have a powerful effect on the men and women around us.

God has a vision, purpose, and plan for each of us. We are all unique in that we have been blessed with individual abilities and talents. Every Christian has been given spiritual gifts or special abilities that we are to use in order to carry out God's plan.

Leadership is a gift. God's plan and purpose has been revealed for us in the Bible. In Romans, you can see where our gifts and purpose are explained to us.

> We have different gifts, according to the grace given to each of us. If your gift is prophesying, then prophesy in accordance with your faith; if it is serving, then serve; if it is teaching, then teach; if it is to encourage, then give encouragement; if it is giving, then give generously; if it is to lead, do it diligently; if it is to show mercy, do it cheerfully. (Romans 12:68)

Leadership is an art. It is the art of accomplishing a mission. As a leader, you must find a way to motivate others to achieve goals. In order to motivate, you need to provide a positive, honest, encouraging, and direct example on a daily basis. A good leader has mastered the ability to command respect but not necessarily demand respect. This is a challenge in itself as respect has to be earned. The way you handle yourself and others can either break or build morale and help or hinder mission success. I believe that it all starts with the example you set as this is what others will see.

Leadership is influence. Great leaders are able to persuade others to think or behave in a certain manner. Great leaders are capable of obtaining results without the use of an obvious force or authority. As a coach, I understand that not all leaders have mastered the art of commanding versus demanding respect. One of the biggest challenges associated with team sports is the achievement of total buy-in by all athletes. Selfish behavior is something that will tear the foundation of the team apart. Dedication, trust, and loyalty are preached, but kids will be kids, and they will make mistakes. At these times, coaches are placed in the position of providing redirection. The application of the proper technique to correct behavior that is unwarranted is a tool in itself and can be used for positive or negative ends.

A coach that understands firm constructive direction and redirection has the potential to make a have a great impact on those around him/her. A coach who utilizes honest, fair, and consistent techniques when dealing with the athletes will be more apt to gain the respect of an athlete than one that consistently uses destructive language and behavior to adjust the athlete's behavior. Consistent, firm, and fair criticism are keys to having positive interaction when a coach wishes to get the most out of the athletes that he/she directs.

Why do people follow a leader? People are pulled to those who have a clear sense of direction and for whom they have respect.

Jesus set the example. He set the tone. Therefore, your example sets the tone! If you want to be a great leader, set a great example. If you say one thing and do another, you are setting yourself up to fail. If you are in a position of authority, you must gain the cooperation and earn the confidence of those whom you are directing. Simply put, to lead others, you must learn to lead yourself. God often reminds me of this. I have to occasionally check myself and my actions. I often ask myself, "Am I a good example for others to follow?"

> Follow my example, as I follow the example of
> Christ. (1 Corinthians 11:1)

> The successful leader not only knows where he is going,
> but has the ability to get others to go with him.

> —the apostle Paul

I AM WHAT I AM

Being self-aware and having positive, healthy self-esteem are extremely important to understanding who you are. By understanding this, you will be more capable of using your gifts and talents as a Christian leader and fulfilling the goals that God has placed within each of us.

Individually, we need to be spiritually self-aware and focused on gaining an inner peace that can only be found by diving into God's word and drawing nearer to God. Once we clearly understand the gifts that we have been given and the calling that God has for each of us, we are then capable of being the person that we were created to be and filling the role that God has in store for each of us.

It is important to understand that each of us is gifted with specific individual leadership traits for a reason. The specific abilities that God has gifted us with are not earned or deserved. Do not think that your gifts will always be there. You cannot wait to use the gifts that God has blessed you with when you feel like it. Understand that if your gifts are not used, they can be taken away. This is why it is important that we identify our role and responsibilities. God has a specific calling for each of us, however, it is a task in itself to fully realize the specific attributes that have been bestowed freely on us. Understand that our abilities have been doled out for the benefit of others. Our abilities are not just for us to use for our personal gain. Once again, this leads us toward a selfish mentality.

Once we realize what gifts you have been given time with God, ask him for guidance, specifically what his plan is for you. Ask him how he wants you to employ your gifts. With the responsibility that God places on us, it is paramount that we place emphasis on and understand the importance of taking proper care of ourselves. Having a strong emotional, physical, mental, and spiritual well-being will allow us to serve others to the best of our ability.

As a leader, we have to be in top form if we are going to provide the guidance to others. I took pride in being a strong, fit Marine. I could run three miles in 18:50. I could easily do two hundred sit-ups in the two minutes that we were allotted and had no problem consistently getting twenty pull-ups during our quarterly physical fitness test. Yet I was always amazed that no matter how much physical training we did as individuals or as a unit, on Fridays, when it was slated that our morning PT session was a company run, I expected to be pushed physically and mentally.

Our company commander took pride in leading this activity. He always seemed to be in top, physical shape and at least one step ahead of the rest of us. This used to drive me crazy. I knew that the CO was easily ten years my senior, and I was certain that I was in better physical shape and had more physical endurance than him, yet every time we went out on a company run, he set the pace, led from the front, and exemplified what the rest of us should strive to be. He ultimately set the tone.

Twenty years later, here I am, a high school football coach. I see permissive parenting, the elimination of punishments in the educational system, and a society that tells everyone that all people are entitled to anything that they want. In more recent generations, we are seeing young people who are graduating high school only to be rudely awakened once they enter the real world and realize that they are not capable of achieving what they hope for because they have not been provided the essential tools needed for success. Sadly, few understand that this is due to a system that has not provided a model of leading by example. So they whine, make excuses, and expect a handout instead of working their way up. We have created a society that has a fragile self-esteem.

I am challenging you to apply yourself. Demand more out of yourself. We must have leaders with a focused approach rooted in core values and beliefs that encompass specific traits and values. Be the tip of the spear. Be the leader that others will follow because they trust in you. Be the warrior for Christ that you were meant to be.

PREPARATION–THE KEY TO MISSION COMPLETION

You are a warrior for Christ. As warriors, we must prepare for combat. As far as most people can remember, there have always been warriors. Warriors are timeless. Warriors live by a moral creed. To be a warrior is a calling because they are not just trained killers; a warrior is conditioned through countless hours of difficult preparation to strengthen both their mind and body.

Warriors will face obstacles. Warriors must have poise when they encounter difficulty. There will be times when a mission is compromised, and the ability to adapt to the situation could be the difference between life and death. A warrior understands that surrender is not an option. Giving up is the equivalent to failing.

Understand that failure is not an option. Our mental and physical toughness is not enough. War fighting must be looked at as an art, just as leadership must be looked at as an art. To be victorious on the battlefield, a warrior must have the fundamental knowledge and be proficiently trained in specific tasks and drills. Warriors must have focus, a strong foundation, and consistent repetition and connection with the details involved in the implementation of his weaponry. When the warrior's number is called, he/she must be ready to deploy, engage, and destroy the enemy in close combat.

The Marine Corps infantry motto, *"The more you sweat in peace, the less you bleed in war,"* is equally appropriate to Christian leadership as it is to a Marine Corps infantry unit. The harder you train, the more prepared you will be for battle. The more prepared you are, the better your chances to succeed when conflict takes place. Tactically, this applies to all athletes and an infantry unit just as it applies to the modern-day Christian leader.

As a Christian who is stepping out to lead, you will face many challenges. There will be times when the devil will try to derail you. There will be obstructions that show up in your path that tests your faith. You will have something going wrong in our life. It is easy to get upset, place the blame on God, and even question why he would allow something like this to happen. Be careful how and on whom you place the blame.

Understand that God never promised us a rose garden and an easy life. What God is looking for are those that will put their faith in him. He needs courageous warriors. It is up to you to recognize the tactics that the enemy utilizes. Adapt to them and overcome. Life's situations are meant to strengthen us individually. Too often, we focus on the fix and do not allow God to move at his speed or on our behalf. So run your race. Know that there will be pain; but fight through the pain, and use the gifts and talents that you have been blessed with. Be victorious for Christ.

COMBAT READINESS ESSENTIALS

The core values of the US Marine Corps are *Honor, Courage,* and *Commitment.*

These powerful words hold special meaning to generations of warriors that have earned the title of United States Marine. These words are the bedrock of a Marine's character. An elite few men and women live by these set of core values. These three simple words guide them in their daily decision-making process. Core values provide order and direct the behavior of Marines. Honor, courage, and commitment are the foundation of the US Marine Corps. Many generations of common man or woman have become extraordinary due to the application of these words into their daily lives.

It would be a safe bet that any organization who roots itself in and stays true to these words will have success. As a coach, I make it clear to those that work with and for me that these three core values are fundamental. My coaches will model these traits every day. If we are to be leaders, we must be steadfast in our premise. If we are not, how can we expect our athletes to follow us?

As one earns the title of Marine, an individual becomes a member of a unit. Within this unit, individuals are committed to each other. Together, these individuals become a force for good. Complete strangers form a bond and stand for something that is bigger than themselves, these individuals form a brotherhood that can meet any challenge and accomplish any goal. The US Marine Corps commitment to these core values is the foundation of the organization's success.

Being a Marine, I pride myself in exceeding beyond limitations that have been set forth by others. As a coach I demand that my athletes strive to better themselves and never accept mediocrity. Think about any average athlete for a minute. No athlete wants to be mediocre. It is the goal of any athlete to be better than the next player. Everyone wants to be a winner. But to reach the pinnacle of success, to be a champion, an athlete must outwork every opponent. If an athlete wants to be the best, that athlete has to put the blood, sweat, and tears into training. Their training has to be twofold. Successful athletic units must train their mind and body in preparation for completion. In order to succeed on the battlefield, a warrior must set aside personal comforts and dedicate himself or herself to the completion of the mission. Just as an athlete prepares for completion, a warrior must prepare for conflict.

The similarities between athletic competition and military conflict are easy to see. In a war zone, in the arena, or in life, sacrifice is crucial. To ensure consistent success, one must periodically reflect on events that have transpired. A dedicated individual will frequently modify his/her approach to reach the goal. Modifications are made so that an individual does not plateau or become complacent. But the crucial element must be that the athlete or warrior stays true to the foundation they are built upon.

As Christians, our mission is just as vital and of even more importance. We live in a world that is heavily focused on individualism. We live in a voyeuristic, narcissistic society that is all about "me." Our culture has become more focused on materialism and pleasure. In modern-day America, we hear "me, me, me" everywhere we go. Our society has become instant where anything and everything that one wants can be purchased or searched up as quickly as one can type on an electronic device.

I like a new car as much as the next guy. I have as much fun while on vacation at Disney World as my kids do, but it is important that we do not get wrapped up in the consumption of goods. Too often, Americans only focus on pleasure. Many people forget that we are unable to take anything that we have acquired with us when we die. I heard on the radio one time, "Our life cannot be focused on the world. Our focus has to be on the word." It took me a long time to understand that phrase, but I can appreciate it now. Prioritization of our priorities is something that we must focus on. Our priorities are a window to our faith.

I grew up in a lower-income family. I never wanted for anything, but I knew that all my friends had bigger houses, nicer cars, newer clothes, and cooler games. As a young adult, once my wife and I started making money, I started purchasing stuff. Why? I thought that having a bunch of stuff meant that I had made it. I felt superficially better about myself. I could look around and materialistically justify success. Nowadays, I realize that success is not determined by the possessions that are owned; rather, success is defined by the legacy that we leave.

I have been blessed with two daughters and an amazing wife. As I have aged and matured a bit, I have refocused my priorities. I now understand that life cannot be about me. I am here for something bigger than "me." God made me for a purpose. God made me to love. I am on this planet to love and support my wife and daughters. Love is not a selfish thing. Love is about sacrifice.

> Watch out for those dogs, those evildoers, those mutilators of the flesh. For it is we who are the circumcision, we who serve God by his Spirit, who boast in Christ Jesus, and who put no confidence in the flesh though I myself have reasons for such confidence. (Philippians 3:2–4)

I have realized that I must deny myself from time to time and be courageous. I will have integrity, strength, and loyalty to something that is of more importance. Why? Because my actions and behaviors dictate the legacy that I will leave.

> "Come, follow me," Jesus said, "and I will send you out to fish for people." (Mark 1:17)

We are charged with communicating the love of Jesus to the world. He will take care of our needs, therefore there is no reason to worry about the little things. Rather, we must pray about the big things. Stand up and put your faith in God. He has your back. He will provide us joyous lives if we just listen and follow his lead.

As Christian leaders, we must be bold. It is our duty to stand up and say, *there is a better way to live*. We have no job that is more important than investing in the future of our loved ones and those that we have influence on. Billy Graham is quoted to have said, "A coach influences more people in a year than most people do in a lifetime." That is a powerful statement, and I believe it. As a coach, you stand in the gap. Our society is in decay, our families are broken, and our children are told that they are entitled to make mistakes. Americans have an excuse for everything. This is unacceptable behavior for all. We must lead boldly. As parents, coaches, leaders, and people of influence, we have to correct and direct anyone that we are able to touch. We must provide the direction and an example for them to emulate.

Not all Christian leaders are the same. If you asked one hundred people to define leadership, you would get one hundred different answers. Expect that there will be many leadership approaches and just as many varying styles. Every leader has a particular style of leadership that is innate. The methods, attitudes, levels of enthusiasm, and behaviors that make one person a powerful motivator may not be effective for the next person.

Learn your style. Great leaders are aware of their own style. If you want to be a difference maker, it is essential that you make an effort to learn how your style actually affects the people around you. A great leader will learn to modify his/her leadership style to reach individual people, groups, and/or organizations. Varying approaches allow for diverse comprehension. In doing so, a great leader is one that is able to learn and apply multiple methods to motivate and inspire. Ultimately, your success comes down to your ability to reach those within your circle of influence.

If we wish to provide guidance, direction, and ultimately help others obtain the gift of eternal life in heaven, we have to be tactically proficient and combat ready. A warrior understands that, as the war rages, he must be able to depend on the man next to him. Our Christian brothers and sisters on our left and right are our warriors in worldly battles. We must have each other's back, for it is our unified front that makes us strong.

Jesus Christ is our ultimate ally because of his amazing leadership. He has provided us an excellent example of true leadership as he leads from the front. The sacrifice he made is more than anyone of us will ever know. He has us covered. He is our shield and will provide valuable insight to defeat the enemy, only if we call on him. There is no better warrior than Jesus Christ. We can rely on his battlefield intelligence. All we have to do is open our hearts and minds in the midst of conflict and let Jesus be our guide. With God's help, we will gain victory over the devil whenever he presents himself.

The Bible informs us of the tactics the devil will use as he wages war. The conflict will be fierce, but this is not a battle of the flesh. We are told that we are actually fighting against demonic forces.

> For our struggle is not against flesh and blood,
> but against the rulers, against the authorities,
> against the powers of this dark world and against
> the spiritual forces of evil in the heavenly realms.
> (Ephesians 6:12)

The devil is a formidable foe. We battle a foe that knows our weaknesses and will quickly shift his attack. For this reason alone, we need to be well rooted in or core values, have strong principles, and base our decision-making on tested leadership traits, for this fight is a fight to the death. However, we should not be afraid. To rephrase military jargon, "Jesus has our six," our back. He is the best backup that we could ever ask for.

CLEAR SIGHT PICTURE

If you are familiar with shooting, you understand that if you want your rounds to hit the intended target, you must have a clear sight picture. In the Marines, you are taught on day one of marksmanship training that a shooter's accuracy is dependent upon his or her ability to align the front sight post in the center, both horizontally and vertically, of the rear sight aperture. A properly aligned and clear sight picture is of utmost importance when shooting. If a shooter does not achieve a clear and balanced sight alignment, the shots will not hit their mark. Great marksmen have excellent focus and fundamentals and make their hits count.

The fundamentals of marksmanship are easily applicable to success in life. An understanding of clear sight picture, in addition to core values, is the bedrock for victory over the enemy. These important fundamentals, traits, and values empower us and provide us the fortitude needed to stand up and advance toward the challenge when obstacles in life arise. When presented with a challenge, fall back on your fundamental beliefs, create a plan of attack, and have clear alignment of your goals and objectives. A clear sight picture will allow you to triumph, for the ability to see your goals is not enough. The fundamentals and framework of shooting can apply to everyday life, just as much as marksmanship.

US Marine Corps training and leadership is based on sound principles. You have to stand for something, so why not focus your sights upon and take a stand for Jesus? If you follow His principles, you can define your character as a leader. Self-evaluation allows you to identify your strengths and weaknesses and constantly seek self-improvement. This analysis is paramount if you wish to be a difference maker. Just as the enemy will change his tactics, you must be willing to adjust and improve upon your personal skill set.

Marines are taught principles of leadership for a reason. A strong leader is a sound leader, and a sound leader is inspirational. From a coaching perspective, a great leader is someone that is consistent. A quality coach must be consistent. Both Marines and coaches must be rock-solid and must not waver through the tough times. As Christian leaders, we must do the same. For this reason, Christian leaders must understand the importance of Christian principles.

It is imperative that we learn and demonstrate strong Christian principles if we wish to draw nonbelievers to Christ.

> Like newborn babies, crave pure spiritual milk,
> so that by it you may grow up in your salvation.
> (1 Peter 2:2)

It is imperative that we spend regular time in the word. In doing so, we gain a better understanding of God, what he expects from us, and allows us to draw close to Him. Just as infants grow into adults, new believers must grow into mature Christians.

Many Marine Corps leadership principles parallel and apply to our Christian walk. If you wish to be a bold, strong, tactically proficient leader that desires to advance Christianity, by incorporating a few of the following principles in your daily walk, you will be able to better guide your actions, your family's actions, and hopefully influence those around you.

Know yourself and seek self-improvement

Be honest with yourself. Do you know your strengths and your weaknesses? What do you struggle with personally? What holds you back or entices you and leads you astray? Some people struggle with addictions, while others have selfish desires. Your personal battle could be as small as loving to eat Twinkies or as big as an addiction to pornography.

It took time for me to personally identify the things in my life that the devil uses to distract me. Spend some quiet time, and self-reflect on your personal struggles. Write down your weak traits. It is important to know your weaknesses because, I promise you, the devil knows where to attack you. He will do anything he can to cause us to lose our way. He will employ different strategies and methods to derail you with aggressive or passive tactics. Once you recognize that which tempts or teases you to go astray, you can fortify those areas, making it is easier for you to fight your personal battles. Most importantly, when you are struggling in a raging battle, lean on Jesus. He will carry you; you are not alone. Remember, Jesus has your back.

Be technically and tactically proficient

As a Marine, one must be competent in his/her military occupational specialty. Marines are required to do their job at a high level, or people die. As Christians, how do we expect to provide our children the guidance and direction that they need or our coworkers the example that they need if we do not delve into the word? It is up to us to read the Bible in order to learn the valuable lessons that are right in front of us.

Being brutally honest, way too many Christians only spend time with God on Sundays. I have been guilty of this in my life. It is easy to lose our connection to God. Our lives get busy, and we can easily lose focus, and/or we just get distracted. I know that when this happens in my life, I have to place major emphasis on spending time with God. Christianity is a personal relationship, not a location. How can we lead others to Christ if we do not personally know him? It is important to learn the word and apply the teaching to our lives, but this is only an option if we focus on your relationship with God. The Bible is full of stories, parables, and teachings that can apply to everyone's life; if we spend time in the word, we can easily find something every time we open the book that applies to our lives.

As a warrior for Christ, we must be a technically and tactically proficient Christians. This is only achievable by studying his word with an open heart and mind. The stories in the Bible are as relevant today as they were two thousand years ago. Just as a coach must understand the ins and outs of the position that he is trying to prepare the athlete to play, we, too, must understand what we are trying to express to others when it comes to God's love. Lives depend on it.

Set the example

Here is the tough part. As a Christian, if we accept the challenge and witness to our lost friends, eyes will be upon us. Everything that we do, our speech, our appearance, our attitude, and our actions will fall under the microscope. Focus our actions, and provide a good witness. When we are around our coworkers or old friends, we will have to stay guarded. Keep our standard high. Make sound decisions and provide an example that will draw others to us instead of people thinking that we are a hypocrite.

As a parent, it is extremely important to not send a mixed message to our children. A strong open relationship with your spouse is important. We have to demonstrate the values and beliefs that we wish our children to embrace. As a parent, I want my children to follow God. I try my best to be a good Christian example for them to learn from. Being a Christian role model at home can be more of challenge than at the workplace. Why? Because our family has a deeper relationship than our relationship with coworkers. Stay strong, stay focused, pray regularly, and keep the faith. In doing so, we can impact our circle of influence. Consistency is the key.

Know your people and look out for their welfare

We have to do more than just tell people about Jesus. Spend time with those we hope to witness. We may be the only strong Christian example that person may ever cross paths with. Make sure your actions reflect Jesus's values. We are powerful. Be evidence for people that we have something different in our lives, something special. Use that God-given strength, and demonstrate what it is like to follow God.

Many people believe that once one accepts Christ as their Savior, it is important to distance themselves from their old friends and find new friends—Christian friends. Many people turn their backs on their old friendships, casting aside old relationships. I cringe when I hear Christians talk about how they can no longer be friends with so-and-so. Christians must cast off our old ways and follow Christ, but this does not mean we turn our backs on our friends. We must be a beacon that attracts our friends to Jesus. Our unchurched friends need to see that there is something different in us. Then, when the time is right, tell them your story. Explain the difference God has made in your life.

We are challenged to live by the word. But as Christians, it is our duty to be the light. This means that we need to mix it up with our old pals. Do not desert them. Be bold enough to spread the good news. This can be tough because there may be resistance. The devil can use this situation to try and slip you up. When you recognize this, pray for strength; however, do not abort the mission. You may be the only person who is able to have an impact on your old relationships.

Develop a sense of responsibility among your subordinates

The people that we come in contact with need to recognize that we are living a godly life. Show them that you are truly interested in their welfare. If they ask about your faith, expound on it. Welcome the opportunity, and take advantage of the time. You may just say something that changes their eternal path. Your testimony is important because it is your story. Everyone has a story, but each story is a unique situation. Use your testimony to open a dialogue with everyone. If the opportunity arises, ask the person about their life. Show genuine interest and make it clear to them that as a person, they are important to you. Be proud of who you are.

Seek responsibilities and take responsibility

Being a good witness will mean actively seeking out opportunities to talk to people about God. This is a challenging assignment. By being brave with our Christianity and actively talking to others, we are actively professing our faith. This is a huge responsibility. By professing our faith, you are opening up personally to others. This is not a common thing in society today because many people are taken back by open, honest conversation. It is important that we stick to our convictions and are willing to accept that some people will be open to what is said, and others will condemn these actions. Treat all equally, and pray for them because we just may not know what may happen.

BATTLE RATTLE CHRISTIAN LEADERSHIP TRAITS

Be completely humble and gentle; be patient,
bearing with one another in love.

—Ephesians 4:2

I will admit that the first time I read this verse, as an adult, I grinned from ear to ear. The majority of people who knew me prior to six years ago would say that those words are the exact opposite of my mentality. Today, I try to incorporate those three traits into my daily life. If I wake up every day with the mindset that I am going to be humble, gentle, and patient, I am off to a great start.

Every day, I place emphasis on the integration of these qualities into my daily life. The process seems to never be complete. I know that I have weakness in my character that keep me from being that man that God wants me to be. I struggle with my gentleness, humility, and patience. I desire to live a godly life, but I have to constantly remind myself that if I want to be more like Christ, I must model these traits regularly.

The great thing about being human is we are not zebras; we can all change our spots.

If you knew anything about the old Joe, you would know that for the longest time, those three words never crossed my mind. Obnoxious, aggressive, overbearing, mean-spirited, and intolerant are descriptive words that better describe the man that I once was. I believe that our experiences are important in developing who we are. For me, the act of being kind is a day-to-day labor in itself. But today, I believe that a real man does not model those traits. I strive daily to be the best man that I can possibly be.

I used to say that the song that epitomized me was, "It's Hard to Be Humble" by Mac Davis. As a young boy, it became my favorite tune because my father would play this song over and over. Even today, I will periodically pull it up and listen to it or share it on social media. I do this half as a joke and half as a reminder to myself that my priorities cannot be centered on my ego. It is a humorous but extremely self-centered song. Listening to it helps me refocus my humility.

God becoming man is an amazing example of humility.

> And being found in appearance as a man, he humbled himself by becoming obedient to death—even death on a cross! (Philippians 2:8)

If God can be that humble, how can we justify our arrogance? From my experiences, I have come to realize that many people who are arrogant are really hiding their inner insecurity.

As a Christian, who are you? What position and responsibilities do you hold as a child of God? The more we strive to have a strong relationship with God, our actions, attitudes, and the words we choose to use must become more thought out. Our actions do represent who we really are. Self-control and especially emotional control are extremely important.

Kindness and patience have to be a balancing act in reference to the Marine Corps and coaching. In our culture, everyone wants to know the "why" when they are instructed to perform a task. In a large group setting, if you are a person in a position of authority and responsibility, the leader does not always have time to answer everyone's question or concern. I have had to develop my own personal leadership style that allows me to accomplish a mission while draining the individual of his/her desire to ask why. This is important in both athletics and in the military because, in times of extreme pressure, we have to act and not question the one that is in charge.

My background as a Marine and as a high school football coach leads me to be more abrasive than gentle. My personal leadership style, as it relates to Marines and athletes, revolves around being "lovingly harsh." I have had to train those around me to respond instantly and with unwavering obedience to orders. A successful Marine or coach has the ability to influence a large number of individuals. This is not easily achieved. Accomplishing this is usually twofold. One must incorporate the use of both positive and negative behavioral adjustments. The process of molding an individual into a unit member can be grueling and frustrating. However, by instilling discipline and structure, a leader can be as demanding and tough on those being lead as long as one demonstrates, communicates, and reinforces a sense that he/she cares for those within the unit.

Think about what we watch on TV. As a society, we worship both warriors and villains as if they are heroes. We love to watch people who push the natural limits. Our heroes are not shy, quiet, or humble. So naturally, we are not either. Additionally, we specifically condition and raise our men to believe that gentleness can be perceived as weakness.

When I think gentle, I think meek. Meekness is not weakness; these words are not synonymous. For me, meek means that I need to have a consistent temperament and behavior. It is a reference that reminds me that I need to hold myself up and act righteously. I try to carry myself in a confident yet controlled manner. In doing so, I am better able to control my emotions and demeanor. If you wish to be Christlike, focus on your meekness.

Meekness, to me, represents strength. Meekness affords us the strength to persevere courageously and patiently. Meekness provides the ability to have self-control. With self-control, we are better able to understand and stand up for the values that we cherish. Meekness is the quality of understanding that we are not overly self-important.

As it is explained in the Bible, if we are to boast, we should not boast of ourselves.

> "But let the one who boasts boast about this: that
> they have the understanding to know me, that

I am the LORD, who exercises kindness, justice
and righteousness on earth for in these I delight,"
declares the LORD. (Jeremiah 9:24)

My lack of patience is one of the avenues that the devil will use to wage war on me. But what is patience? Patience is having the ability to endure and carry on when we face difficulty in life. I have noticed that when God wants me to grow a specific quality, he puts me in the exact opposite circumstance so that I must focus on my actions. God is presenting me the opportunity to learn from the situation. I know that God provided me with two daughters so that I would become a more patient man. I believe that God uses my strong-willed girls to mold me into a better form of myself. I have learned a lot about personal self-control as I persevere through difficult situations. By learning more about myself, I learn how to better deal with the daily trials and tribulations that I face in life. Patience is a virtue, and my meekness allows me to be a more patient man.

It is human nature to be more patient with those we work with or our friends than we do with our own family members. I am guilty of this in my life. This may be attributed to the fact that I hold those closest to me to a higher standard. I expect more from and out of because of the close, personal connection that I have with my wife and children. I have also learned that I must show more self-control when dealing with those who mean the most to me. Why? Because God expects more out of me. But when I slip up, he does not come down on me with his full wrath. Instead, God teaches me by example and is meek and patiently steadfast in how he redirects me.

JJDIDTIEBUCKLE AND JESUS

The first time I read Ephesians 4:2 and saw that Christians need to be humble, gentle, and patient, I instantly went into flashback mode. It was as if something clicked, and in my mind, I instantly rattled off the old Marine acronym JJDIDTIEBUCKLE. JJDIDTIEBAUCKLE is an acronym that is regularly referred to in the Marine Corps. Each letter represents one of the fourteen leadership traits that form the backbone of Marine Corps leadership. Each trait is individually instrumental in explaining the decision-making process when a Marine takes a course of action in garrison or on the battlefield. Additionally, these traits significantly impact the way we carry ourselves in our day-to-day lives. For these two reasons, every Marine is required to memorize, recite, and incorporate each into their daily life. Once a Marine, always a Marine.

I think so highly of JJDIDTIEBUCKLE that I have a large poster and outline of each specific trait hanging on the wall in my classroom. The first week of school, I give my students an assignment where they are tasked to learn each trait and how each can be applied to their life. I do this in hopes of providing influence that will have a lasting effect on their decision-making process. The next generation needs character development. School cannot be just about standardized test scores. Character development is something that is more and more overlooked as important, so I make it a priority in my classroom and athletic programs.

The fourteen leadership traits in JJDIDTIEBUCKLE are *j*ustice, *j*udgment, *d*ependability, *i*nitiative, *d*ecisiveness, *t*act, *i*ntegrity, *e*ndurance, *b*earing, *u*nselfishness, *c*ourage, *k*nowledge, *l*oyalty, and *e*nthusiasm.

Ask any Marine or any of my former students what this acronym stands for, I would bet you that they can rattle it off.

Jesus is my shepherd. Jesus said, "I am the good shepherd. The good shepherd lays down his life for the sheep" (John 10:11). Jesus described Christian leadership in this verse. Leaders are to act as shepherds. A shepherd is trusted with a lot of responsibility, and a shepherd's job is never done. A shepherd must direct, protect, feed, and correct the flock that he has influence over. Christians have to be shepherds that model righteousness and godliness in our daily lives, for we are the example that others see.

> Follow my example, as I follow the example of
> Christ. (1 Corinthians 11:1)

We have been challenged by God himself to be the example and provide the inspiration that sparks others' interest in him.

The Christian leader must be a guardian as shepherds provide protection. The shepherd acts as the eyes and ears of the flock. In relation to humans, there are predators that search out and identify sheep that they wish to entice them away from God. The predator uses weapons, like newspapers, magazines, and the internet, to supply false and misleading facts. The enemy uses a constant barrage of lies in order to deceive us. Satan is a powerful foe who is a brilliant tactician. He uses every technique and tactic that he has in his bag of tricks to lure us in hopes that we will bite.

The devil's hand has made its way into very influential areas of our culture. His work is easily discernable in the political cookie jar and in the classroom. He has infiltrated and is directing many in political office to use and abuse their position. These so-called leaders have a governmental pulpit to push an anti-Christian agenda. Even worse, Satan has gained a stronghold of influence over our children.

There are many teachers in our educational administration, as well as the classroom, that use their position of authority to influence the future of our nation by rewriting our books and inputting a liberal agenda that is tearing at our nation's fabric and history to shreds. It is our duty to provide defense for those close to us if we want to give them a chance to survive. Open your eyes. I am begging you to see the power that Satan's influence has on the world around us.

If we are lax and allow America to continue down the path it is on, we may lose a few sheep or worse lose the entire flock. Jesus warned us, "Watch out for false prophets. They come to you in sheep's clothing, but inwardly they are ferocious wolves" (Matthew 7:15). As Christian leaders, we must boldly stand up for our beliefs and our values.

Mental, physical, and spiritual preparation is essential if we are going to provide security and support to the individuals in our flock. The leadership traits in JJDIDTIEBUCKLE provide a reference that the Christian leader can model his/her leadership around. Not only will understanding the leadership traits of JJDIDTIEBUCKLE and applying it to our daily walk provide a foundation to help us in our daily lives, but if Christians embrace the following qualities and incorporate them into our daily walk, just as Marines do, the American Christian can become a powerful agent of blessing that can make an eternal impact on lives. For we are God's warriors, and we are fighting an enemy that shows no mercy.

JJDIDTIEBUCKLE:

Justice

Justice is the practice of being consistently fair. Justice is also the act of giving reward and punishment impartially, according to the merits of the case in question. Personal accountability is important. How can someone expect others to do what is expected if he/she is not disciplined enough to do the same? As a football coach, I must hold people accountable. I must constantly observe the actions of the coaches that work for me and the athletes that play for me. As a coordinator, it is my job to make sure that each are performing the duties that they are tasked with to their utmost potential. It is important that each person understands that if they act accordingly, then reward will follow. If poor decisions are made, they have to be held accountable. Coaches may be promoted or demoted just as an athlete's performance may allot movement up or down the depth chart.

As a coach, it is important that each player, no matter what his or her individual role, is equally held to the same level of accountability. As a Marine, it is important that each individual is rationed tasks that are both difficult and easy to perform uniformly. The Bible states, "Do not judge, and you will not be judged. Do not condemn, and you will not be condemned. Forgive, and you will be forgiven" (Luke 6:37). I have learned that to keep moral high, merit and consequence have to be passed out fairly. As Christians, we need to make sure that we are acting godly in our authoritative role. No one is perfect, but our actions and decisions are being observed, judged, and critiqued. Not all of our decisions will be good ones; everyone makes poor choices from time to time. If you have reservations on an issue or a subject, pray to God for guidance before you make a major decision. He will provide the guidance and direction that you need to help with the answer.

Judgment

Leadership entails the acts of assessing and directing. To make a sound judgment, one must weigh facts. By weighing facts and looking at multiple possibilities, one is better able to produce measured actions.

It is important to understand the effect that our decisions will have on others. As a Marine, sound judgment in the decision-making process is important as you are often assigned the responsibility of tactically employing small units. Thorough decision-making is essential in this process if you wish to succeed in your endeavor. Think about our recent conflicts in Iraq and Afghanistan. Many of the missions were special operation missions. Small unit planning, organization, and application had to be thoroughly thought out. Why? Because once the small unit of six to twenty men would be inserted behind enemy lines, and these units were relatively on their own without any support or backup, success or failure would be determined by many of the decisions that the team leader made on the ground while in the middle of battle. Sound decision-making is not only determined if the team's mission was a success or failure, but failure could ultimately result in no one making it home alive.

As a coach, I have had to rely on my judgment when dealing with athletes that consistently make bad decisions. This process is not an easy one, and I have found myself facing tough decisions. Do I get rid of an athlete, or do I allow the athlete to stay in the program? Love and grace play into the decision-making process, and this is where the struggle begins. Every athlete has a different story and background, so a coach cannot respond to each situation the same. But if a coach allows an athlete that constantly makes poor choices the opportunity to stay in their program, he/she is inadvertently sending a message that if an athlete continues to choose poorly, they will always get another chance. So a dilemma emerges. How can a coach demand that the rest of the team follow the rules if a particular athlete can a get out of trouble-free card? By allowing the athlete to remain, I could be the source of inconsistency that is harmful to team chemistry. Grace and punishment both play a vital part. Just as God provides grace, he will punish us as well.

One difficult aspect of leadership is that the one who is responsible to make the decisions has to be able to weigh the pros and cons accordingly when thought-out decision-making occurs.

> Teach me knowledge and good judgment, for I
> trust your commands. (Psalm 119:66)

Falling back on this value, I try and turn to God in the process and ask him to provide me with the wisdom to discern right from wrong so that I may make a sound judgment.

Dependability

A person must be dependable because dependability and trust are synonymous in my book. American culture is battling with the dependability aspect. Everywhere we look, someone is swindling, lying, or stealing something. Everyone wants to get ahead in life, but very few people really want to work for success. High school football in the great state of Texas is an excellent opportunity for young men to understand the importance of dependability and success. In any Texas town, on any given Friday night, you have violence, trash talk, screaming parents, a band playing from the stands, yelling coaches on the sideline, and a quarterback or linebacker barking out the offensive or defensive call for each play. Football is an excellent opportunity for the next generation to learn the importance of depending on the guy next to you in a stressful situation. Stress and the ability to deal with stress are of major importance in life. This is a perfect setting for a sixteen- or seventeen-year-old male to grow. If an athlete is selfish or lazy just for one moment, the entire team pays for the mistake.

As adults, we feel stress every day, but how we deal with it makes all the difference. Look at the US Marine Corps. The Marine Corps has the most stressful and profoundly intense boot camp in the world. The Marine Corps has created this high-stress, high-tempo environment with a reason in mind. Marines understand that in combat, there is chaos. And when thrown into an intense situation, performance is a necessity. Valuable lessons are learned when one deals with situations that have confusion and mayhem. In either setting, on the gridiron or on the battlefield, the ability to make quick decisions and perform under pressure is a necessity. Because of this, a person must be dependable.

Marines demand that each individual is dependable on and off the battlefield. Football players listen for the play call and do their individual job. It is all about trust. Dependability is being able to count on the man in the trenches next to you. In the arena of life, when times are tough and the pressure is on, we rely on our bond with others to get us by. We depend on those that will go the extra mile for us or properly perform their prescribed duty unselfishly.

I trust that God is there for me in the difficult times. He has made it clear to me that he has my back. I know that when difficulty arises, I can always call on his name, and he will be there for me.

When I am afraid, I will trust in you. (Psalm 56:3)

Initiative

Each of us must find a way to take initiative. In life, we will be placed in situations where leadership is not just important; it is crucial. Do not be confused about initiative. Initiative is not about personal glorification. Initiative is about taking charge when there is a void that needs to be filled. Taking action in the absence of orders for personal recognition or for glory is not necessarily a good thing. Personal initiative is useful when you identify a lack of or an absence of leadership. Sometimes you must take it upon yourself to do what is necessary in order to accomplish the mission. Improvise, adapt, and overcome! This is the Marine Corps way. This is what leaders do.

Initiative can be good and bad. The overwhelming need to attack a challenge and not wait for someone else to do what you believe needs to take place can backfire. Initiative can lead to personal problems for the person who thought they were making a sound choice. I will admit that I struggle to control my need to express my personal initiative at times. I have to temper myself regularly. I have the potential to micromanage any situation that I feel is in need of direction. In my twenty-two years of coaching, I have come to recognize that as much as initiative can be a good trait to have, it can also hurt you. If something needs to be taken care of and there is a void of leadership or direction, there have been instances where I have taken the initiative to lead and make the command decision because someone has to.

When I see things that I believe needs to be addressed, I tend to address them. Sometimes I throw tact out the window. This is not always a good thing. I have realized that I do this because of my background. I believe this urge to fix things comes from my experience in the Marine Corps. However, in the civilian world many people struggle with or do not know how to take someone who is wired in this manner. I understand now that my sense of initiative is a positive but at times is a negative aspect of my character. But I am thankful that I have been able to see my weaknesses. This allows me to work on fixing them.

We hear that some among you are idle. They are not busy; they are busybodies. Such people

we command and urge in the Lord Jesus Christ
to settle down and earn the bread they eat. And
as for you, brothers, never tire of doing what is
right. (2 Thessalonians 3:11–13)

Decisiveness

To accomplish a mission, you must understand your challenge. It does not matter if you are game-planning for a sports competition or setting up a tactical raid in hostile territory. Maybe you have been placed in charge of creating a major presentation, and you will go in front of your company's board. It is imperative that you have a goal set before you start on your mission. Identify which available resources you must utilize and understand which methods you must incorporate and employ to ensure success. I recommend that you have a secondary plan in place that addresses obstacles that may present themselves along the way. A thorough plan will include multiple contingency plans that you may use to overcome these impediments. Then, when the time comes, be decisive.

How is one supposed to be decisive when they are forced to look at all the elements listed above? Just thinking of all the planning that must take place can easily overwhelm anyone. It comes down to time allotment and time management. Timely decision-making is just as important as sound decision-making. Plan smart, but plan wisely. If made in haste, inferior decision-making can lead to an operational downfall. However, there are times in life when we must act. In war, speed is the essence of success. But most of us do not live in a war zone, and in life, we must have a balanced approach to planning.

For me, a strong enemy daily engages me. Satan constantly looks to derail me. He attacks my thoughts, emotions, and actions. I have to make quick decisions that can affect how I respond in that moment. Will my response be positive or negative? I am better prepared today than I was a few years ago, but I will still respond in a reactionary manner. This can lead to negative outcomes down the road even if I make these choices with good purpose. So I have learned to weigh the facts and information surrounding the situation I am in and make a thought-out yet timely decision.

I still make mistakes. At times, I fall short and fail, but I am still striving to be the best godly man that I can be. I learn from my actions and reactions. I apply what I have learned to the next assault and take the battle to the enemy. I will provide the leadership my family needs and deserves.

> But if serving the LORD seems undesirable to you, then choose for yourselves this day whom you will serve, whether the gods your ancestors served beyond the Euphrates, or the gods of the Amorites, in whose land you are living. But as for me and my household, we will serve the LORD. (Joshua 24:15)

A good leader must possess the courage to act. The person that is entrusted with command has to begin the planning, create a plan, operate the plan, and attack the objective. It is important to understand the correct operations that must take place and the steps that must be taken. The leadership element must have the internal fortitude to confront any challenge in the path that has been taken. This is why leadership is difficult; it takes courage. Despite the difficulties that you will engage along the route, overcome adversity and complete the mission. Decisiveness of action is just as important as having the courage to act when you are in a leadership role.

While in combat, a squad leader who identifies a potentially dangerous situation must quickly create a plan and decisively take action to prevent an attack or injury from occurring because the mission matters, but lives are at stake. As Christians, we must make up our mind to serve the Lord. We must make the decisive choice to lead because Satan will ambush us when we least expect it. We cannot become complacent. We must have situational awareness.

> I know your deeds, that you are neither cold nor hot. I wish you were either one or the other!

So, because you are lukewarm—neither hot nor cold—I am about to spit you out of my mouth. (Revelation 3:15–16)

Tact

Tact is one of my weaknesses. I seem to struggle with tact in my everyday life because I have discovered it is one of my weaknesses. In the past, I have allowed my lack of tact has hurt my personal relationships and my professional life. As a young man in my twenties and thirties, I was a hotheaded loose cannon. People around me never knew how I would react to any given situation. I was an arrogant and conceded man whose actions kept people on edge. Many of my previous actions and comments had pushed friends away. As I have aged, I have gained greater control over my emotions. Today I focus a considerable amount of effort on self-control. I believe that if I want to have control over my life and be an influence in other's lives, I must have tact when communicating.

How does tact apply to leadership? Tactful people have the ability to communicate in a way that allows others to understand the message or meaning in a inoffensive manner. A tactful leader decides the language or behavior that will be utilized when directing people. Tact is a skill that enables one to work with others without causing conflict. A good leader has the ability to understand the mood and atmosphere that he/she is working in. Why is this important? Leaders' choice of words can have a positive or negative impact on a situation. Our spoken words have an effect on people's perception and reaction in a situation. Words can be catalysts. Words can cause a spark, but is the spark lighting a fire for good or bad?

Plain and simple, tact is the ability to deal with others in a manner that will maintain good relations. This involves knowing how and when to say things. When I speak to others about faith, I need to think about what I am saying and take a tactful approach. If an opportunity presents itself that affords an avenue to talk about Jesus to relatives, coworkers, classmates, etc., incorporate a tactful approach. I think through what I want to tell this person. Do I not lecture people or provide to take an approach that could give them a false impression? I try to be honest and genuine. It is important to think through what I want to portray and consider how my words will come across. I look for an opportunity to show God's love but try to be considerate of predisposed opinions, knowledge, or beliefs that many people may have.

> To slander no one, to be peaceable and considerate, and always to be gentle toward everyone.
> (Titus 3:2)

I try to remember that this may be the only opportunity I have to help someone that I am speaking to gain eternal life.

Integrity

Honor and integrity go hand in hand. Integrity and honesty are powerful words in relation to values and belief systems. People hear what you say verbally, but what you do physically has an impact as well. We have all heard the profound statement: Your actions speak louder than words. Our actions have influence. An integrity-driven leader must hold true to his/her values. Be the example that you desire out of your employee, child, friend, coworker, Christian brother.

It is commonly believed that "a man is only as good as his word." Your integrity is your honor; it is one of the things that people cannot take away from you. We live in a world that gives very little value to honesty and integrity. Sure, our leaders talk a big game, but look at the state of affairs in our political system. The people we elect to represent us are lacking in both honesty and integrity. It makes me sick. This integrity-inspired leadership void trickles down to the lowest levels of employment.

> Whoever walks in integrity walks securely, but whoever takes crooked paths will be found out.
> (Proverbs 10:9)

I am currently a defensive coordinator in a major Texas football program. When I look to hire coaches on my staff, I look for people who have sound integrity. I try to research a perspective person's background and see what their foundation and beliefs revolve around. I look at their social media accounts, and I do an Internet search on them. A high school football coach will impact many lives, and I refuse to hire and work with any person if they are a person of low integrity. Some people think this may be a little over the top. I have been told, "What people do in their own time is their own business." I say, "Bull corn." This is an extremely important job. As a high school football coach, your livelihood revolves around influence. Our job is all about accountability, commitment, integrity, and the ability to buy into a system and give everything that you have to the team. Without integrity, you do not have a unit. You have a group of selfish, self-centered individuals who are only looking out for themselves.

A coach must set high expectations, demand conformity to a set of rules, values, and teach the importance of commitment. If the athletes know that the coach is a man of low integrity, they will not follow his rules or him. If a coach demands commitment and accountability out of his players, he must model this in his speech and actions. Success revolves around trust. Integrity equals trust. As coaches, businessmen, pastors, and fathers, we are blessed to be in a position where we are entrusted with molding lives. We must have uprightness of character and soundness of moral principles. Our words and actions impact and influence, and anything else is unacceptable.

Endurance

Endurance is a window that reveals the level of mental and physical stamina a person has and illustrates our ability to withstand pain, stress, fatigue, and hardship. Having the internal fortitude to complete anything that you have been tasked with is essential. Your ability to overcome adversity and endure when others would rather quit is important because it shows others what you are made of. Endurance is an important leadership trait.

"Embrace the suck"—this is a phrase that is commonly used in Marine infantry units. The meaning behind the phrase is simple: What you are about to do is going to suck, and a common man would want to quit. The thing that makes you special is that you understand and realize that you are able to push through the pain and finish the task. It serves as a reminder that you are mentally tough enough to endure that hardship, overcome the fatigue, and surpass failure. Endurance allows you to push through the pain, adapt, and to do whatever it takes to complete the mission.

The enduring leader understands that if a job must be done, then it is his responsibility to get it done. As a football coach, if I do not have the pads, dummies, chutes, or equipment available at a particular time, I simply adapt my coaching approach, drills, and techniques. I always get the job done because an enduring leader will find a way.

As a Marine, there are times when the best or appropriate gear that is needed to accomplish the mission is unavailable. Marines understand this and do not complain. Instead, we laugh about the situation as a way to relieve stress or frustration. We take pride in doing our job better than the unit that is better equipped. It really defaults to personal pride and responsibility. No matter what, finish the job. If that means you have to be a verbal inspiration to those around you, then provide the motivation needed so that others get it done.

In 2014, I participated in a fundraiser in Dallas, Texas, for families of veterans. During the event, I carried my one-hundred-pound. backpack for forty-three miles in seventeen hours. The final ten miles were completed with a gas mask to restrict my air intake by 30 percent. This was done in hopes of inspiring others to donate to a worthy cause. My feet were devastated. I literally shredded my toes. In all my years of running and road marches, this one event had the most profound physical effect on my forty-year-old body. But I endured; I accomplished the mission. Why would I do such a thing? This was an opportunity to use my talents and gifts as an influence. I physically and mentally "embraced the suck" for a cause. I was a member of a team that raised nearly $30,559 that year in support of *heroes* that sacrifice for us on a daily basis.

> Not only so, but we also glory in our sufferings, because we know that suffering produces perseverance; perseverance, character; and character, hope. (Romans 5:3–4)

Bearing

Bearing is the manner in which you conduct and control yourself. As a Christian, how do you conduct yourself? Do you have good bearing? From time to time, we all will lose our bearing. Your appearance, posture, and the tone of your voice all say a lot about who you are. Are you someone who is known for self-control and self-confidence? Challenge yourself to provide the example for others to follow through your actions, attitude, and behavior.

As a Christian leader, do you have a distinct purpose? Do you read the Bible regularly and habitually focus on the Lord, or are you a Sunday morning Christian? If you wish to be a good witness, you must continually push and search for self-improvement. By obtaining a deeper understanding of what God wants for us in life, we are better able to comprehend how we are to go about reaching our goals. As a Christian, people are always observing your actions. Your bearing reflects your mental discipline and self-control.

It is important that our bearing provides a favorable impression on others. Remember, other Christians will be judged by our appearance, carriage, and conduct. Our true feelings are expressed in our actions. If you look like a duck, walk like a duck, and quack like a duck, you must be a duck. If you are going to provide leadership and direction, you must look, talk, and act the part, or people will think you are a phony. Romans 12 makes it clear that we should not conform to the world but be transformed. We say we are Christians, but do we act Christlike on a daily basis?

> Jesus Christ is the same yesterday and today and forever. (Hebrews 13:8)

Unselfishness

Are you someone that looks out for the needs of others? In the Marine Corps, the unit leader always eats last. This is done to ensure that there is enough chow for the men in the unit. This action by officers and noncommissioned officers may not seem like much, but it is done with purpose. Letting your troops eat first is an example to the men in the unit that their individual needs and comforts come before the welfare of the person who is in command. This example of unselfishness reassures the warriors that their leader will sacrifice personal comfort for those who do the work in the trenches. The first example of selfless leadership I can remember took place in Marine boot camp while we were doing field training. It was our first day, and we had just finished setting up our tents. The drill instructor informed the recruits that it was time to assemble for chow. I observed that our leaders ate last. Later I learned that "leaders eat last" was a Marine Corps leadership expectation to ensure that the troops were taken care of first.

A quality leader is unselfish. As a Marine, it is important that a leader looks out for the people they command. As a head coach, you have to do the same with your assistants. In doing so, you gain the respect of the people you work with. Your subordinates will work harder for a person that cares for them and goes out of his or her way to ensure their personal issues are of value.

An unselfish leader will step up when difficult situations arise. It is important in gaining trust that you look out for the welfare of others. However, the unselfish leader understands that this must not cloud your ability to accomplish the mission. It is important that you stay focused on your goals and continually make progress toward your end point.

When I think about the ultimate act of unselfishness and sacrifice, I think of Jesus bearing the weight of the world's sins on the cross. There is no way that we can possibly comprehend the weight that Jesus must have borne on his shoulders as he carried the sins of all of those who were alive at the time of his death, who are alive today, and people who are yet to be born. As humans, I do not think we could ever be conscious of the depth of his selfless act for humanity.

> For God so loved the world that he gave his one
> and only Son, that whoever believes in him shall
> not perish but have eternal life. (John 3:16)

I often refer to Christ's unselfish act as inspiration for myself.

Courage

Courage is not the absence of fear but the ability to press forward when you recognize it. Courage is the inner strength that propels a warrior to take that first step and charge into battle. Courage is what allows that student athlete to tell his friends, "*No*, I will not do drugs" at the party. Courage is doing what you believe is right and required of yourself because you wish to stay true to your values. Courage is what allows a Christian to speak up when something is spoken in a situation that is not acceptable, even though the actions may cause a personal setback.

If your priorities are more important than your personal comfort, there may come a time when you have to stand up to an advancing enemy or be the one that will speak out in a crowd. Far too many people are unable to find courage when they feel pressured or uncomfortable. Find your inner strength and refuse to back down from a fight or shrink into a corner. God has empowered each of us with the ability to speak up and speak out. If you wish to be the Christian leader that you are capable of being, you will need to prepare yourself for confrontation. The enemy will set an ambush and attack when you least expect it. Identify your inner fear because that will be the target of the attack. Face your fear head-on and conquer it. The difference between being a hero and a coward is the ability to overcome the fear in our mind.

Think of the fear the apostles must have had when they left Jerusalem and journeyed out to herald the news of our risen Lord. These were ordinary men, but they traveled far and wide to share the good news in a religiously hostile world. Due to their bold witness, many suffered greatly and, in many cases, met painfully violent deaths. These were all average people, yet they refused to run from their fear. Instead, these ordinary people "Embraced The Suck" and spoke up for Christ. These spiritual warriors accepted the challenges and punishments for stepping out in the face of popular disfavor and ultimately paid for it.

Fighting and winning wars, especially religious ones, can be dangerous work. Jesus knew that his followers would be confronted. Jesus knew that the apostle's mission would send them into hostile territory.

> He said to them, "But now if you have a purse, take it, and also a bag; and if you don't have a sword, sell your cloak and buy one." (Luke 22:36)

I think this was Jesus's way of telling his apostles that there would be dangerous times in the near future, and they had better prepare themselves for whatever lay ahead. Each and every one of the apostles was attacked and persecuted by the enemy. This is a reminder to me that I must stay vigilant, be prepared, and courageous.

Knowledge

If you desire individual success in any endeavor, you must be knowledgeable in the activity you are undertaking. Leaders, however, must understand that in order to have unit success, a level of personal familiarity with your team members is crucial. Individually, anyone can learn a group of specific facts that apply to a job. When achievement depends on having to rely on the person on the left or right of you, I suggest you have an understanding of whom it is you are working with. Who are they? What do they know technically? But most importantly, what motivates and inspires them?

Invest in the personal and technical development of your team. The more knowledgeable your team members are, the better off you will be. You have to provide those that you count on with the information that is needed, opportunities to grow, and to develop personally.

If you are in a leadership position, do not hold onto all of the knowledge; this is not leadership. This is giving direction. No one wants to work for a control freak. If you want people to work well for you, you have to give them something to work for. Allowing some individualization is not an act of giving up control, rather this allows the people in your unit to gain ownership in the business.

When people feel as if they have ownership, they will work harder. If one has a personal connection to the process, the end result will mean more to them. The best leaders provide knowledge and direction but afford the individuals within the team an opportunity to run with the ball. At this point, the leader becomes a manager/adviser, one who can provide feedback on how the person is doing and what might need to be modified to ensure success. An example of this is how I lead my defensive assistant coaches. I provide an in-depth, outlined defensive scheme with specific drills that must be incorporated into individual drill time. Besides the specific drills that must be worked on, I allow my coaches to incorporate any drill that they believe is helpful for the athletes. Why? Because assistant coach needs to have ownership in the process. Individual ownership allows an individual to coach passionately and more profoundly.

As I coordinate the defensive side of a football team, I have a mission. I have a systemic foundation that must be installed and a specific set of expectations that I want accomplished. Proper sequential steps have to be taken that must be accomplished. If this is not done properly, the defensive unit will not succeed.

Coaching football is not a one-man job. I rely on four men as assistants to help me coach up to sixty athletes every day. I have to provide my coaches with the knowledge that I want them to impart on the athletes. As the defensive coordinator, I put my coaches through a weeklong version of "coach's school." As a staff, we meet for eight hours a day to ensure that we are all on the same page. It is imperative that my coaches understand the defensive philosophy. I express that there are position-specific, nonnegotiable skills and rules that must be taught to the athletes. At this time, I lay all of the essential information out for my assistant coaches. We cover the coaching/mission essential specifics to ensure we are all on the same page. As a staff, defensively, we must present a united front and use the same terminology. I make it clear that I do not like to micromanage and allow each individual coach the opportunity to adapt fundamental drills as they feel needed to put the athletes in the best position possible to secure victory on game day.

> So we say with confidence, "The Lord is my helper; I will not be afraid. What can mere mortals do to me?" (Hebrews 13:6)

The same thing applies to our faith. If we dive into the Word, we are blessed with a deeper understanding of how to live our lives and how to witness to others. We become an equipped warrior for good. Just as a basic Marine must know how to use his individual weapon, a seasoned veteran has been trained and gained expertise on multiple weapon platforms. This well-versed warrior learns how to operate each of the other weapons in the arsenal of his rifle company. Listen to God. Open your mind, and listen to what he has to tell you.

Loyalty

I once read a story about the leadership of Grace Murray Hopper, a US Navy Rear Admiral. She once said, "Leadership is a two-way street, loyalty up and loyalty down. Respect for one's superiors. Care for one's crew." Leaders show loyalty by providing support for and tending to the care of those under their command. Junior members of an organization show their loyalty in return by efficiently carrying out the instructions and orders they have received.

"Semper fidelis" and "Always Faithful" pretty much sum up loyalty in two words. Marines show unwavering loyalty to each other, their traditions, and heritage. Pay attention the next time two Marines meet. Even if they are from different generations of service, there is an instant bond and understanding being that each is a member of "the brotherhood." It is understood that, should either ever be in need, they can always count on a fellow Marine to have their back.

Marines who have been told to clean the latrine will enthusiastically carry out the order, though they may internally oppose the duty as a church member/friend volunteer to help fix the lighting in the church sanctuary when asked on a Friday night, even though he knew it would take three or four hours to complete. Each example describes an expression of loyalty to someone or something. When someone is loyal, they are being faithful. For me, Jesus Christ is the perfect example and is the spiritual embodiment of "Semper fidelis."

I rejoice that my God is a faithful God. Jesus Christ guides me, provides for me, and protects me when the times are tough, and the devil is attacking me.

> No temptation has overtaken you except what is common to mankind. And God is faithful; he will not let you be tempted beyond what you can bear. But when you are tempted, he will also provide a way out so that you can endure it. (1 Corinthians 10:13)

It is stated in the Bible that God will not allow us to endure more than we can handle. When we feel as if the burden is too heavy, God tells us here that *he* will provide; all we have to do is call on him for backup. Jesus will swoop in like a military QRF, quick reaction force. Jesus will never forsake us. He will stand side by side with us and provide the strength that is needed in difficult times.

> He will cover you with his feathers, and under his wings you will find refuge; his faithfulness will be your shield and rampart. You will not fear the terror of night, nor the arrow that flies by day, nor

the pestilence that stalks in the darkness, nor the
plague that destroys at midday. (Psalm 91:4–6)

Enthusiasm

Attitude is everything! As a Marine, I spent a lot of time in the ocean. One of my Marine training instructors would comment every time we would hit the beach and prepare for a two-kilometer open ocean fin that if you want to perform to your potential, you had better start with your mind. He would say, "Your attitude will dictate your success. Your attitude throughout this exercise is everything." He was correct. My attitude, how I mentally attacked the training, dictated how I felt during and after the training took place. As a coach, I constantly remind my athletes that they must show up every day with the proper mindset. Why? Because if you want to succeed at anything in life, you had better attack every day with the proper mindset, and you had better be enthusiastic about it.

If a person is enthusiastic about something, that person will be more willing to persevere through difficult times to prevail. I embrace an enthusiasm approach to my job. I show up every day with a smile on my face. I make a point to pat a few athletes on the back, tell a few of them something positive about their appearance, or crack a joke on a couple. Occasionally, I pick on an athlete and have a one-on-one dance off with one of them in front of the team. Why? I want the athletes to be excited to be a part of the program.

As a Marine, I spent hours upon hours perfecting mission orders, mission planning, asset coordination, and controlling the movement of personnel and equipment in small unit and large-scale missions on the battlefield. Similarly, as a coach, I have spent countless hours to gain the knowledge that is needed to successfully lead a group of seventy young men on the gridiron. Success, in both arenas, relies heavily on the unit's will to trust in each other and the leader.

Enthusiasm and inspiration go hand in hand in leadership. An enthusiastic leader has to be able to quickly recognize any negative views, comments, or positions. He must act swiftly and shift the focus to positivity. This is not always an easy task to accomplish, but a veteran leader will consistently reference enthusiasm and use it as a probe. Enthusiastic leadership will often lead to enthusiastic behavior by those you are able to influence.

A quote I like to us as a motivational tool is, "When the going gets tough, the fun is just beginning!" because success is dictated by how you are going to respond when adversity shows up. More importantly, what is your mindset in relation to the barrier that may be in your way?

As a leader, it is important to recognize when the internal motivation starts to dwindle. Think of motivation as a way to restart a fire in a firepit. All you have to do is stir up the coals in the bottom of the firepit, add some tinder, a little spark, and *blam*, the flame will ignite.

When your team is down by three touchdowns, and the athletes have a look of despair at halftime, are you capable of providing the inspiration that is needed to ignite the athletes internal will to fight and *win* the game? Use enthusiasm and turn the *can't* into a *can*!

As a Marine at the school of infantry, we would go on long conditioning hikes. Most of these hikes consisted of us wearing full battle rattle and an eighty-pound pack. I vividly remember one twenty-mile forced march. I saw a strong Marine go out of his way to pick up the pack of a weaker Marine that was falling behind. Our company had just started up a steep hill climb when this Marine with strong leadership traits snatched the pack up off the deck and carried the eighty-pound ruck to the top of the hill while singing out cadence as he ascended up the hill. I was proud to observe such a profound example of enthusiasm. The energy became contagious, and it motivated the struggling Marine to dig deep and find strength that he did not know he had to finish the climb. It was an amazing example of how enthusiasm can be inspirational.

Enthusiasm is a powerful leadership trait because it is contagious. Let your light shine!

> Where, O death, is your victory? Where, O
> death, is your sting? The sting of death is sin, and
> the power of sin is the law. But thanks be to God!
> He gives us the victory through our Lord Jesus

Christ. Therefore, my dear brothers and sisters, stand firm. Let nothing move you. Always give yourselves fully to the work of the Lord, because you know that your labor in the Lord is not in vain. (1 Corinthians 15:55–58)

Maybe our enthusiasm for Jesus could ignite a flame in someone. Maybe that someone will be a difference maker for Christ.

As a Christian, mental, physical, and spiritual preparation is essential if we are going to provide security and support. The leadership traits in JJDIDTIEBUCKLE provide a reference that the Christian leader can model his/her leadership around. I hope you refer back to JJDIDITIEBUCKLE when you feel as if you need to lead, shepherd, or provide protection to the individuals in your flock.

I am a major fan of JJDIDTIEBUCKLE. I refer back to it frequently. The incorporation of JJDIDTIEBUCKLE into my life has profoundly impacted many facets of my daily decision-making process. My personal foundation has been strengthened. I have made an effort to live by a set of core values, and these traits significantly influence on the way I carry myself daily. Each of the fourteen traits can easily be incorporated into or lives.

JJDIDTIEBUCKLE provides a solid leadership foundation for any coach, teacher, or minister. They work just as well for any small business owner, a CEO, or a father/mother. As Christians in leadership positions, we can become a powerful agent of blessing and have an eternal impact on lives. Remember, we are God's warriors, and we are fighting an enemy that does not believe in mercy. These fourteen leadership traits provide the mental, physical, and spiritual preparation we need to support and defend our flock.

INDISPENSABLE KNOWLEDGE FOR THE COMBAT EFFECTIVE CHRISTIAN LEADER

Creation vs Evolution

This will not be another talk about which came first, the chicken or the egg. I am not going to try and explain the debate between the big bang theory and "let there be light." I am going to try and explain my take on "nature versus nurture" and how I believe it applies to leadership.

If you ask one hundred people their opinion on leadership, you will get one hundred different answers. Some people believe that leaders are born while others believe that leadership is developed. Let's relate leadership and the idea of "nature versus nurture" to leadership development. There is generally a three-way divide in relation to human development. One group believes that humans are born with all of the specific traits and characteristics they need in life. Another group believes that our experiences in life train and teach the skills needed for our success. There are a good number of people who would agree that a combination of traits that we are born with and the lessons that we learn in life mold us into the adults that we end up. In other words, I am the man I am today because God made me this way, but the path that I have taken in life has influenced my character development and decision-making ability. So Joseph Welock is a combination of "nature and nurture."

I do not believe that great people are born great. I do believe that God has blessed each person with individual traits that, if developed, allow certain individuals more achievement than others. Some people use their God-given talents and some do not. My life experience tells me that each of us are individually shaped by the unique circumstances that we go through in life. These experiences, plus our talents, determine our potential. At one time or another, each of us was just a face in the crowd. The few that stand out from the crowd are the ones who are able to recognize the situation that they are in, observe the people around them, apply what life has taught them to the situations that present themselves in life, and ultimately achieve greatness. As for the negative experiences, great people do not just throw away the negatives in life. Great people learn from the negative experiences he/she encounters. They reflect on what happened in these situation so as to apply them if similar circumstances arise in the future.

In our lives, we will interact with thousands of people. These interpersonal relationships and interactions assist us as we develop into who we are as adults. Each time we deal with another person, we gain something from the interaction. Not all of our personal relationships are positive, but each provides us necessities to refer back to and to learn lessons. This learning process is the part that I believe is a crucial ingredient in the leadership development process.

In the US Marine Corps, when a recruit shows up for boot camp, he or she is instantly disconnected from society and reality. Upon entering the gate at Marine Corps recruit depot, the process of stripping the individual away from each person begins and ends once the thirteen-week process of Marine building ends. At the end of the thirteen-week boot camp, every single person leaves the depot a member of a new family, mentally and physically stronger and better equipped to engage any obstacle that may present itself to them.

The US Marine Corps is 100 percent focused on building warriors, but the Marine Corps mission is based on creating leaders. The most important thing that today's young men and women learn while in boot camp is leadership. Each person is thrown in a team environment where they not only learn about each other and that they must learn to depend on each other for success, but they quickly identify their own strengths and weakness and are pushed to improve upon those that need the most attention.

As athletes enter into the high school football program from multiple middle schools, they are instantly forced to work with new coaches, learn a new philosophy, and are introduced to new teammates. One of the first steps is learning how to work with and compete against a new group of athletes. It is important for these athletes to understand that in order to be successful, they must come together quickly, develop into a tight unit, and push toward and sacrifice to achieve the same goal.

As a coach, I often reflect on my experience growing up in athletics and my time as a Marine. I try to look at what the athletes are going through and use my experiences to develop relationships that help them reach individual and unit goals. As I coach, I am ultimately focused on helping them develop into tomorrow's leaders, fathers, and husbands.

General Cates, nineteenth commandant of the Marine Corps, stated, "Leadership is intangible, hard to measure, and difficult to describe. Its quality would seem to stem from many factors, but certainly they must include a measure of inherent ability to control and direct self-confidence based on expert knowledge, initiative, loyalty, pride and sense of responsibility. Inherent ability cannot be instilled, but that which is latent or dormant can be developed. Other ingredients can be acquired. They are not easily learned. But leaders can be and are made."

I believe that God provides each person with a specific set of skills and traits for a purpose. However, I also believe that should you not use the gifts or traits that God has provided, he is also able to take the gifts away from you and award them to another person.

I am of the school of thought that our individual experiences can have a lasting effect on what we become. Recently, I coached a linebacker who, during his junior year, only touched the field in one game and only during the fourth quarter once our team was ahead by twenty-four points. No high school coach would ever think of him as a leader if they saw him on the street. In the eleventh grade, this young man was a short, light, and relatively weak athlete. After his junior football season, this same athlete focused his direction and attention on one thing—becoming a leader. He believed that it was his time to step up as a vocal leader on the team. He became the powerful spark that could unite eleven individuals into a tight-knit unit. December through July, this young man lived in the weight room. By the time we put pads on and started two-a-days in August, he had become a man. He learned to take any false step or any mistake that he made personally and grew from it. He had developed into a vocal leader and led by example. This athlete developed into the glue that held the defensive group together.

As a senior, the athlete that barely touched the field became an all-district linebacker who was one of the top five in the state for tackles. He had caused more fumbles than anyone that I had ever coached. This young man was on a mission to develop into a leader. His team looked up to him, respected him, and inside, many wished they could have played like him. Why? Because he took what he had been given and increased it. It was an honor to be a part of his development, and I am proud of the man that he has become. He has a bright future ahead of himself. Today, he is a success. He is a fireman in Dallas, Texas, married, with two young daughters.

There is a potential greatness in everyone. As Christians, we must look at the circumstances that surround us, and apply them to who we are as well. Greatness comes from hard work and preparation. I do not believe that you must have the correct DNA, but I believe that everyone can better himself or herself. Sometimes we just need to provide a little push or a nudge to inspire evolution.

Think about Saul of Tarsus. Saul was an enemy to Christianity. He was a persecutor of and a relentless pursuer of Christians who made it his mission to find and jail believers of Jesus Christ. He was stopped in his tracks one day while on the road to Damascus. He was about to experience a life change, and he never saw it coming. Jesus Christ had a mission for Saul. His new mission was to become a powerful messenger, a leader for Christianity.

I am amazed at how God can change our plans. At any time, God can show up and throw a speed bump in front of us, shake us up, and redirect our path. The event that transformed Saul into Paul was immediate, but the process of preparation for the job ahead was a long one. Once redirected, Paul spent close to three years in obscurity. This time period must have been extremely difficult for him. He was an outcast to the Jews and not trusted by the Christians.

It took God a long time to prepare Paul in preparation for his new Job. Paul became an amazing man, but it did not happen overnight. Once God had prepared him for his position, Paul traveled throughout the land, preaching salvation to the Gentiles. Paul went on missionary journeys and persevered in the face of danger and persecution. Paul and his transformation from enemy to ally has been a source of inspiration for countless missionaries throughout history. I am amazed that God could change an enemy of Christianity into a champion for the cause. Today, Paul is referred to as one of the all-time leaders of Christianity, but this was not the only time God used developing leadership. God is all about developing leaders. He did the same thing with Moses; God sent Moses to the desert for forty years to prepare him for his responsibility.

Before his change, Saul was referred to as a Hebrew among Hebrews, an extremely knowledgeable religious person who prayed all of the time. He was said to have a brilliant mind, knowledge of both philosophy and religion, and renounced as a skilled debater. Saul was no dummy; he was an educated man.

These attributes and his history may have been the perfect combination that Jesus Christ was looking for to fill his leadership role. We must remember that God can change anyone. God threw Saul a curveball. When Jesus revealed himself to Saul on Damascus road that day, Saul was blinded for three days. I believe that the three days of blindness are important in that they provided a period of internal struggle before Paul's rebirth as a leader of the church. In correlation, Jesus was resurrected after three days.

I think that Paul's endowed gifts, when focused in the correct direction, provided a powerful force for good. His experiences, strength, and wisdom, provided Paul the endurance to carry out the mission Jesus presented to him. As Paul said, "I can do all this through him who gives me strength" (Philippians 4:13).

Paul pressed forward to accomplish his mission. Paul is credited with writing thirteen of the twenty-seven books in the New Testament. By spreading the gospel, his efforts yielded strength and encouragement to the early Christians in a hostile time. If Jesus Christ can take Saul and transform him into Paul, then what can he do with us? Maybe we should open our hearts and mind a little more and listen for direction.

God has shown us how we can transform and develop ourselves into strong Christian leaders that he needs through the conversion of Paul. Paul became a preacher that spread the gospel and taught that people are saved by the grace of Jesus Christ and not by our works. Thank you for developing strong men like Paul, and thank you, Jesus, for sacrificing yourself so that we can have eternal life. Today, we can rejoice in our salvation because of your power.

> For it is by grace you have been saved, through
> faith-and this is not from yourselves, it is the gift
> of God. (Ephesians 2:8)

FORTIFICATION DUE TO CONSISTENCY

Do you think of yourself as Rambo, a modern-day superhero, or are you as tough as a high-speed, low-drag, special operations ninja assassin? In today's world, we watch television or stare at the screen of some handheld personal device 24-7. We live in an era that is so caught up in the fantasy world that many have lost touch with what it takes to be strong. Or society thinks that they are tough because they play tactical video games. In reality, our society has lost its edge. Many in society lack the fortitude or mental toughness to push through obstacles in life. It seems that every time I go to a store, I see men walk around with a permanent frown on their face. These men carry themselves as if each and every one of them could easily be the next cage-fighting world champion. But in reality, it is all for show.

This persona or facade is just an act. Are we all really tough guys? Or are all these men just trying to fool the next man to cover up our internal deficiencies? I ask this question because I believe America has turned into fantasyland. We live in a society that is unbelievably focused on toughness. Yet our society is focused on portraying ourselves as something or someone that we are not. Just look at what people post on social media. People only post positive pictures so people think highly of them. I believe we have completely lost touch with reality in our search for acceptance.

It is 2016, and everything we want is within our grasp. We can instantly order whatever we desire online today and have it delivered tomorrow. We can watch a video about any subject matter that we choose on our smartphone and quickly become a pseudoexpert on the subject. More and more people believe that they are special and entitled to something for absolutely nothing. We are so caught up on equality that everyone seems to believe that they should have access to everything equally without working for it! The problem is we are surrounded by *wannabes* that live in a world of dreams and do not want to achieve. These people just want instant self-gratification without putting in the work. The generation that I currently coach and teach is lost. That is why I take leadership development personally. Someone has to stand in the gap.

We currently have a generation of young people who lack a sense of true identity. Our educational system believes that every student should follow the same curriculum and that every student should graduate and go to college. We no longer place value on or teach technical skills. Our educational system is cutting the budgets for music, arts, or mechanics. More and more focus in being placed on test scores due to the fact that school performance dictates funding. Today's students are being overloaded by ever-increasing standardized tests that seem to account for everything. I see students every day that cannot read a common wall clock and are unable to complete simple math without the help of a calculator, but our system has them taking calculus and chemistry classes that have teachers passing them through due to accountability standards and fear for their jobs. In the near future, I believe we will have an entire generation of uneducated college graduates who battle for low-paying jobs.

I pray every day for the world that my two daughters will live in once I am gone. For this reason, I focus on preparing them to succeed in a time when America is no longer the nation it is today. I think it is very important that my daughters develop high self-esteem. I teach them that nothing worth having is easy or free and that they will have to work for everything they get in life. The things we cherish and take the most pride in are the things that you have had to sacrifice for.

Our society is lacking the character, morals, and the internal fortitude that allows us to face an overwhelming situation. Strong people attack any and all situation as if it was a challenge and triumph due to sheer pride and resolve. We must change our way of thinking and doing if we want America to stay on top. As Christian leaders, the time is now. We have to speak up for values, morals, and ethics.

Every day I reflect on my actions and ask myself, "Did I provide an example of mental toughness for my daughters and my athletes?" Some days I am happy with myself, others I am disappointed. When I think mental toughness, I think of consistency. The quality of being consistent is an outstanding attribute and one that I try to embrace every single day. As a Marine, as a coach, and as a father, I strive to be consistent in my actions. The best compliment anyone can say about my work ethic is that no matter what is happening personally in my life, I am consistently the same person, working at the same level of professionalism with the same amount of enthusiasm every single day.

I pride myself on professionalism. If I say I'm going to do something, I do it. If I say I'm going to be somewhere at a specific time, I do everything that I possibly can to be there. I believe a man's mental strength and self-discipline can easily be measured by looking at his level of accountability on a daily basis. As an individual, success will require doing the things that others are not willing to do. Consistency is a must, whether we are working in a vehicle repair shop, developing people, or cultivating a business.

Mentally tough people are not weak-minded. Mentally strong people make a habit of consistently managing their thoughts and behaviors. Strong-minded people do not feel sorry for themselves. You have to evaluate the circumstances that currently surrounded you, pray over the situation, listen for guidance, and open a door for yourself. Never throw a pity party; God does not like weakness.

Mental toughness does not mean that you have to attack every problem the same way every time. You do not have to barrel through every obstacle in the same manner. Be open to change. Be flexible, and listen to others around you. Learn to be adaptable to any situation, and have faith in God's direction. I know that God can adapt our path at any time he feels necessary. Do not be reckless, weigh the risks and benefits of any situation, but strive to make the best choices that you possibly can for the right reasons.

Recognize that you are not in control. Place your focus on the things that can be controlled in life. Be a strong example for others to follow, even if that means that the only thing we have control of is our own attitude and our prayer life. You are not going to please everyone. Speak up for your beliefs, and stand firm in your resolve.

Consistently doing the same thing repeatedly but consistently coming to the same conclusion is ultimately a waste of time. Learn and grow from the mistakes. Accept responsibility for your actions or behaviors, and adapt your plan of action. Acknowledge your failures, but do not relive your past, be it good or bad. Instead, move forward and make better decisions the next time you are faced with the situation. Come up with a game plan, and adjust for the future. Stay rooted in your beliefs while adjusting your focus. This will allow you to strive diligently toward your goal.

Do not allow negative thoughts to consume you. It is important that you do not get caught up with selfishness or jealousy. I know, when I struggle with jealousy, I pray for strength. This is something that I have consistently found to help in one of my personal areas of weakness. These thoughts can easily knock me offtrack. Continually look for opportunities to further yourself and your beliefs. It is critical that you do not allow other people's feelings or frustrations to affect our day-to-day attitude.

Remember, our individual success is determined by our ability to do the things that others are not willing to do on a consistent basis. Mentally strong people make it a habit to consistently manage their thoughts and behaviors. Challenge yourself to be consistent in your faith and walk.

> Finally, brothers and sisters, whatever is true, whatever is noble, whatever is right, whatever is pure, whatever is lovely, whatever is admirable— if anything is excellent or praiseworthy—think about such things. (Philippians 4:8)

MUSCLE MEMORY

When you hear someone speak about muscle memory, often they are talking about how a person is able to eat with their eyes closed or type on a keyboard without looking. Think about an athlete that is able to perform the same maneuver repeatedly and perfectly. In the military, a sniper is able to squeeze the trigger smoothly and flawlessly on a rifle by repeating the same marksmanship fundamentals while executing the same movements over and over again. Muscle memory is the act of training yourself subconsciously to repeat an action without actually thinking about it.

If you are a shooter, you may have heard of the importance of muscle memory and how it affects your accuracy. The ability to have a consistent trigger press is an example of trained muscle memory. A slow, steady, reliable press of the trigger is crucial to trigger control. Most shooters will dry fire their weapon countless times to train their body to be consistent. Many believe that to be proficient, you must train your body repeatedly to prepare it because, when the time comes for action, you do not have time to think; you must act. A professional shooter is not able to recall the hours spent training his fundamentals, nor will he be able to recall the number of times they have pressed the trigger while dry firing a weapon or firing live ammunition. However, each of these actions are done in preparation to hone the shooter's skill in an attempt to train the marksman's finger press. Repetition and muscle memory are what allow the shooter to achieve the perfect press.

As a Christian, we have to make a habit of reading God's word. In a similar fashion, we have to gain the knowledge and acquire the mechanics that enable us to take the proper steps when we are pressed into action. Individual preparation comes into play here as well as in marksmanship. If we wish to have a closer relationship with God, we have to allot time for Bible study. This will allow us to develop into strong Christian leaders and ultimately succeed when the time comes for us to act.

As disciples for Christ, we must understand how our past experiences can help others. If someone comes to you for advice or support, the ability to relate to others helps you aid those who are going through a difficult time. For this reason, I personally believe that some of the best religious leaders are those who have traveled through their own "valley of the shadows." Our individual experiences provide a reference point and a potential connection when trying to relate to people who are hurting. If you have familiarity to a cause or effect that surrounds a behavior, you may be more capable of understanding the stress or emotions of others and better able to provide relevant guidance.

Be consistent if we want others to foresee you as someone to genuinely trust. With all the eyes on us as professed Christians, it is imperative that our actions create a muscle memory of their own. This allows the people around us to better identify our expectations due to the modeling that they observe.

COMMUNICATION

How are your communication skills? I ask this because one's ability to effectively communicate makes connections with others, and growing relationships is important. There may come a time where you find yourself in a position where people search you out for advice. A good communicator has an ability to detect and react to people's feelings and needs. If people rely on you for guidance, you had better be ready to help them fight in their battles against the enemy. You are one of God's most valuable assets, and you will find yourself under attack as well. Your ability to communicate God's word immeasurably adds to your ability to aid people as they maneuver and try to survive tough times. But the time spent in God's word will also strengthen your own spiritual foundation.

> But God has surely listened and has heard my prayer. Praise be to God, who has not rejected my prayer or withheld his love from me! (Psalm 66:19–20)

You have to be able to communicate to lead. Communication is an art in itself. Hone your communication skills, and learn how to relate to and propel people to perform. Dedicating time daily to studying the Bible twenty minutes a day will greatly benefit you. See it as a force multiplier. Time with God not only helps you grow, but it also reinforces your core values and mission. Express to those around you the importance of doing the same in their own life. This is essential when communicating expectations.

If you want to lead, you had better be comfortable with constant decision-making. People will look to you for answers and direction. You will become a compass that keeps those within your circle of influence on target. Use your position as a decision maker to facilitate action. Provide the inspiration needed. The best way to facilitate action is to lead from the front. Be active, but give others the power and authority they need to grow. Be sure to empower those around you through opportunity.

> Everyone who competes in the games goes into strict training. They do it to get a crown that will not last, but we do it to get a crown that will last forever. Therefore I do not run like someone running aimlessly; I do not fight like a boxer beating the air. No, I strike a blow to my body and make it my slave so that after I have preached to others, I myself will not be disqualified for the prize. (1 Corinthians 9:25–17)

Allowing others the opportunity to lead is crucial because opportunities allow people to grow. By allowing opportunity to control a situation, a leader is able to assess the knowledge level, attitude, and drive of those they work with. Additionally, you can assess the strengths and weaknesses through their interaction with others while in a position of authority. Just as the military deploys troops, it is important to understand the depth of the talent pool that you have and think through the proper placement of each person.

Use the knowledge you acquire, and provide feedback. It is important to know your colleague's capabilities and knowledge level. Communicate your thoughts, and have them reflect on and help with any adjustments that need to be made. Do not let anyone leave feeling defeated. Energize them! Reinforce that you have faith in their abilities. Communicate in a way that will inspire movement forward. Without feedback and reflection, growth is difficult to achieve. Good leaders do not believe in being comfortable or allowing the people around them to be comfortable. Stay on your toes, and make sure that the people whom you count on do the same.

Leaders are teachers. Successful leaders are not afraid to get their hands dirty. Never forget where you came from, and do not make the mistake of thinking that you are above doing anything. This type of attitude will easily dislodge any connection that you may have.

Repetition creates muscle memory in gun fighting just as opportunity and evaluation ensures people are consistently developing the tools, training, and support needed to succeed in any position. If people feel as if they have worth, they are more apt to apply themselves wholly for you or your organization. Help people stand out above the crowd.

> In everything set them an example by doing what
> is good. In your teaching show integrity, serious-
> ness. (Titus 2:7)

COMPLACENCY KILLS

We cannot play it safe in life. If we do, we become one of many sheep in a flock. Christian leaders better remember that the wolf is hungry, and he is ready to devour you. Most people want a car that gets outstanding gas mileage. Some people refuse to grasp an opportunity for advancement because they are scared to fail, but playing it safe can be more dangerous than taking risks.

Too many people refuse to take a leap of faith. We must not hold back. Rather we must constantly drive forward. If we are passionate about bringing people to Christ, we will have to step out of our comfort zone. Stepping out of our comfort zone will open opportunities that we may not have opened up before. I am not talking about opportunities for advancement. I am talking about opportunities that may have eternal impact. Be aware that this could mean that we may be taking a few risks along the way.

It is important that we find and unleash our personal passion. Strengthen those around you. Find someone close to you, and ask them to become your accountability partner. Make sure that this person is someone who will call you out if you lose your way or start to slip. Make a pledge to God and to yourself and to your accountability partner that you will hold each other accountable. By holding each other accountable, you are acting on the account of the other person and holding them responsible for their actions. Everyone needs a *Bible buddy* to keep them in line and on path. All warriors need a battle buddy, someone that you can call on or who will call you out when you slip up. My Bible buddy has changed from time to time, but I am thankful that today I have a small group of like-minded Christian men that will call me out when I lose my way.

We don't always get what we want in life, that is why we need a Bible buddy. Things do not always pan out the way we like. Your Bible buddy needs to be someone that you can call, text, or email when you need support. This person can help solve problems and provide guidance in dealing with circumstances that come up. I recommend that this person not be your spouse. It needs to be someone that can look at situations that are presented in a more objective way, from a different perspective.

When you decide to pick your Bible buddy, you need to make sure that this person understands the importance of respect, communication, and accountability. There will be times when you will have to listen, provide support, and give feedback from a nonjudgmental perspective. At times, you will not like the advice or opinion that you receive, but you want your support structure to be honest. A Bible buddy is not someone who will coddle you. This person will be there for you, but his/her role is to ensure that you stay on track.

What stops good people from becoming great? A lack of hunger stops most people from progressing. Complacency kills! Human beings can easily become complacent, which is a dangerous thing. Comfort can lead to poor decision-making. As a leader, too many people rely on you and your decision-making for you to relax and play it safe. Eyes are on you all the time. If the people around you trust your leadership, they will follow your actions. You cannot afford to relax and become lazy. The stakes are high, and you need to have that person who will call you out and put you in check. Refuse to play it safe, and do not become complacent. Playing it safe will cause you to lose the respect and trust of those around you.

Have a backbone, and confront problems. Do not be afraid to take chances. Calculate the risk, but make sure that you understand an important part of leadership is risk-taking. Just remember that you have to be accountable for the actions you have taken. If you are a coach and invest in T-shirts, mugs, and yard signs to be sold at sporting events, you had better make sure that the right people are placed in charge of selling and accounting for these items. If you are a leader at a church and you decide to invest in bounce houses to use at community functions, be aware that you are going to have to make sure and stay on top of the community calendar so that you can use your resource.

Complacency applies to the church as much as it does business. Kalyn Brassfield, a pastor at Elevate Church in Murphy, Texas, does an outstanding job with community outreach. Elevate Church is involved with every city event, music festival, or fair that takes place in the city. The church uses bounce houses as a way to present itself to the community and provide a service to the community. Church members volunteer to put up, work, and take down the bounce houses. Throughout the event, nothing is really said about Christ or salvation, but it is pretty clear that Elevate Church is providing the entertainment for the children. A level of commitment and sacrifice is involved in doing this; but if it saves one life, it is worth it.

Our children are our future. We cannot be complacent when it comes to getting them into church. In my opinion, the best way to get children involved in church is to supply them with fun and exciting learning environment. If the kids have fun while they are at church, they are more apt to want to return. I have seen kids beg their parents to return to Elevate. By getting the children excited about coming to church, you are able to involve family. The family legacy is the important part of the whole process. If God is not a part of the family, the devil is knocking at the door. He wants to rip apart families and will attack the children as well as the adults.

Have you become a complacent leader? If you feel that you have relaxed your focus or have become lazy, search out a Bible buddy. Start now and change your course of action. It is never too late to correct your path. Correct your heading, and move forward. We do not have time to be complacent. Rest is for the weak. Refuse to be a weak Christian. God depends on you.

I came across a story while reading an online devotional a few months back. The story is focused on a poor woman who felt compelled to visit a large, beautiful church near her apartment one Sunday. She did not have much money and wore a T-shirt and jeans to the service. One of the deacons noticed her, went up to her, and welcomed her but made a point to inform her that she needed to go home and speak with Jesus about what she should wear when she came to church next Sunday. The deacon informed her that people who attended church here wore a suit and tie or a dress. The following Sunday, the lady returned to church and wore the same T-shirt and jeans. The deacon once again made a point to ask her if she had spoken to God about what he believed she should wear to church on Sunday. The lady's response was that God had informed her that *he* did not know what she should wear to that church because *he* had not been there in a long time. I love this story because God does not care about what we look like or what we wear. God caries about our heart and our mind and wants to use us, no matter what we look like or where we live.

It is extremely easy to lose focus and get all wrapped up in petty things that do not matter. I believe that is why God spoke of meekness. We have to constantly focus on our ability to be humble, patient, and honorable in our thoughts and actions, for it is easy to lose our way. This is a great example of why I firmly believe that everyone needs a Bible buddy who will call them out and make sure that our priorities are in order. We all need someone in our lives that will speak up and be a voice of reason before the snowball starts rolling downhill.

TRUTH AND HONOR

Trust is a word we hear every day. Trust me, trust us, trust them, blah, blah, blah, blah, blah. What are you actually doing in your life that would motivate someone to gain trust in and have faith in you? If you are in an environment that revolves around teamwork, a great way to instill trust is by incorporating team-building exercises into office meetings or the team outings. Trust, however, is something that must be earned over time. Trust is something that you have to build.

Genuine trust cannot be earned by spending one afternoon playing catch or basketball with your coworkers. Trust is something that you develop over time. Common trust is developed in a group by repeatedly taking care of, sacrificing for, and working with others. A leader's ability to break down preconceived walls between employees is extremely beneficial. This can improve the atmosphere in the workplace as well as promote the health of the business. A leader's ability to bring a diverse group of people together and pursue a common goal is critical for success. This is crucial to moving ahead, especially if you want to grow over the long haul.

Having common goals gives management and staff something to work toward together. This can improve morale on both ends, increase trust between different levels of workers, and keep management in touch with the employees they are responsible for supervising. Bringing staffers into the process of setting and achieving common goals makes them feel valued and more invested in the success of the business. This is a tremendous morale booster that will show in employees' interactions with each other, management, and customers.

Think about Jesus. He had twelve disciples. These people were chosen to represent Jesus in lands far beyond Jerusalem. This extremely diverse and average group of individuals traveled the world to tell people everywhere the wonderful story and promises that God was giving for humanity.

> Jesus went up on a mountainside and called to him those he wanted, and they came to him. He appointed twelve that they might be with him and that he might send them out to preach and to have authority to drive out demons. (Mark 3:13–15)

These twelve individuals spent time together. They ate together, studied together, and sacrificed together. They formed a bond and believed in each other. This group of individuals became God's ambassadors for the kingdom of heaven to the people of the world. These very average individuals became a special group of allies for Jesus. These people were more than just students; they were all chosen for a special purpose.

> But you will receive power when the Holy Spirit comes on you; and you will be my witnesses in Jerusalem, and in all Judea and Samaria, and to the ends of the earth. (Acts 1:8)

Trust is about having faith in someone or something that is bigger than you. Knowing that you can trust in someone to have your back that is focused on the same goal can be greatly beneficial when it comes to completing a mission.

> But I trust in your unfailing love; my heart rejoices in your salvation. (Psalm 13:5)

I trust in the Lord with all of my heart. I cannot explain how appreciative I am that he sacrificed himself on the cross to die for the sins of the world. In doing so, he has gifted us the opportunity to live with him in heaven for all of eternity. Thank you, Jesus, for taking those twelve common individuals, empowering them, and developing them into Christian leaders. The time spent with Jesus, the things they were taught, and the amazing miracles that Jesus performed were instrumental in developing deep trust.

God is a constant companion to me. I am thankful that the relationship we have as father and son is as strong as it is. By providing feedback and reinforcement every day, I know that *he* loves me, and I trust in him wholeheartedly. I may not always like the feedback that God gives, but I listen and try to correct my actions. I do not always want to hear what he has to say, but his feedback is what makes the personal relationship so powerful. I trust that he is providing sound advice. God is alive, and he is there for us whenever we need him.

> Trust in the LORD with all your heart and lean not on your own understanding; in all your ways submit to him, and he will make your paths straight. (Proverbs 3:5–6)

Too often, we get caught up in little moments of life or the momentum of work that we lose sight of what is really important—our relationship with God. Recently, I have thought a lot about how I honor God in return for all that he has given me. I try to honor God by diving into his word because the act of reading and applying God's word helps me draw near to him. In doing so, I honor him. The societal norm is that life is too busy. Life can easily distract us. When this happens, we lose focus on *him*. It is extremely easy to place something in front of reading the Bible, pray to, or talk with God. How many times do we find an excuse for why we do not spend time with God?

Honor refers to the value that we place on a specific ideal or person. What one person places value in, he usually holds in higher esteem. Honor originates deep within our hearts. We show God respect when we honor him. In doing so, we are demonstrating that we love him, value him, and hold him in high regard. We have to do more than just honor God outwardly. God wants honor to come from our hearts.

> The Lord says: "These people come near to me
> with their mouth and honor me with their lips,
> but their hearts are far from me. Their worship
> of me is based on merely human rules they have
> been taught." (Isaiah 29:13)

There are times when I do not give honor to God and have even dishonored God with my actions, but I recognize my faults and strive to do better. I have discovered that the more time I spend with God, the more clearly I hear him. Our relationship is stronger when I am closer to him and he uses me as a more productive resource and tool to further the faith. I have also come to realize that the more I drift away from God, the less I feel connected to him. This absence and distance allow me to live life more selfishly and ultimately provide opportunities for the devil to squeeze his way in and wreck the relationship even further.

The more I honor God, the more He honors me in return. The better my relationship with my wife becomes, the closer I connect to my children, and the more possibilities open up professionally. This leads to a give-and-take relationship. I do right; I am rewarded. I recognize the connection, and I try harder to honor God for what he has provided. But then there is the human aspect that slips into the equation.

> Husbands, love your wives, just as Christ loved the
> church and gave himself up for her. (Ephesians 5:25)

I know my weaknesses. I must do a better job of ridding myself of selfish indulgent desires. The more I praise and honor God, the more blessings he pours out on me. It really comes down to my mindset. I have to choose to give honor to the one who has provided everything to me.

> Love the LORD your God with all your heart and
> with all your soul and with all your strength.
> (Deuteronomy 6:5)

I am blessed beyond measure. I am not lucky. I have not achieved what I have on my own. It has been given to me for reasons that I truly do not understand, and I do not deserve any of it.

I am forty-nine years old, and I am blessed with an amazing life. Most days, I do not understand why I have what God has given me. I have been all over this world. I have been places most people would not want to go in this world. I feel regret every day for some of the things that have taken place in my lifetime. I feel shame for many of the actions as a young man, but I thank God every day for his grace. For all that I have been blessed with, I am thankful. I make a point today to do a better job of showing my appreciation by honoring God more profoundly. I am thankful for Jesus's unfailing love. He has "Covered my 6" and provided the help and support I need at times. It is my duty to repay him for all that he has done for me.

By honoring God, I am doing my part to maintain a two-way relationship. It is my duty to vigilantly search out new ways to be the witness and the example that he wants me to be. I have not always taken advantage of the opportunities that he has presented to me as I look to stand in the gap. As a younger man, my actions were not that of a Christian leader. Since my focus has been adjusted, and the focal point has been placed on God, I am able to more easily recognize the opportunities he places in front of me. I use these moments to seize the opportunities to repay his kindness by being the man that I am supposed to be.

> If we confess our sins, he is faithful and just and
> will forgive us our sins and purify us from all
> unrighteousness. (1 John 1:9)

Thank you, Lord, for all that you do. I will honor you.

BULLET RESISTANCE

re you built to last? When the battle rages, will your armor hold true and protect you? What are your defenses made up of? As a Marine, I have utilized many different forms of firepower to rain down destruction on a host of diverse targets. I will tell you that not all people, metals, earthen bunkers, and vehicles are built the same. If you take an AK-47 and fire two hundred rounds at a regular vehicle, the vehicle will look like Swiss cheese by the time you are finished. The penetration will be thorough. The rounds will enter one side and exit the other with very little problem. However, if you take the same AK-47 and fire it at a reinforced, up-armored vehicle that can withstand an assault, you will have a completely different result. The type of metal and glass that is incorporated into the up-armored vehicle provides a bullet-resistant factor and an elevated level of security that will defeat the flurry of bullets that are fired at it.

If you follow Christ, honor him, and stand up for him, you will come under attack. Each of us will be ambushed as we traverse the mountains and valleys of life.

> When Jesus spoke again to the people, he said,
> "I am the light of the world. Whoever follows
> me will never walk in darkness, but will have the
> light of life." (John 8:12)

The word of God is a light for your pathway. It is important that actions and motives are focused on the light, but we must be prepared for battle. We must prepare for the attack. On one hand, it is just as important to be prepared for an assault.

The whole armor of God

> Finally, be strong in the Lord and in his mighty power. Put on the full armor of God, so that you can take your stand against the devil's schemes. For our struggle is not against flesh and blood, but against the rulers, against the authorities, against the powers of this dark world and against the spiritual forces of evil in the heavenly realms. Therefore put on the full armor of God, so that when the day of evil comes, you may be able to stand your ground, and after you have done everything, to stand. Stand firm then, with the belt of truth buckled around your waist, with the breastplate of righteousness in place, and with your feet fitted with the readiness that comes from the gospel of peace. In addition to all this, take up the shield of faith, with which you can extinguish all the flaming arrows of the evil one. Take the helmet of salvation and the sword of the Spirit, which is the word of God. And pray in the Spirit on all occasions with all kinds of prayers and requests. With this in mind, be alert and always keep on praying for all the Lord's people. (Ephesians 6:10–18)

As a Marine, I have been around a good number of type A personalities. There may be no other place in the world that is as crammed with as many competitive, Greek god-looking, egocentric, and hardheaded men. I have seen a good number of men who looked the part but were not battle ready. There are a good number of Marines who look like the perfect physical specimen, yet a decent number struggle to pass qualification courses or indoctrination programs that would afford them to reach the pinnacle of warrior status.

A lack of proper preparation for the adversity that they are up against sends them to a tactical grave.

Marines are amphibious warriors. Marines spend a great deal of time in the pool and the ocean. One would be surprised how many men swim like fish in a pool but struggle in the ocean. There are those whom you would never think would succeed in the surf who excel. Due to cable television and Internet video streaming, there has been a false identity associated with and a belief that every Navy Seal and Recon Marine look like Arnold Schwarzenegger or the comic book character Thor. When in reality, the vast majority of warriors who run far and swim farther look as if they are more suited for long-distance running and shaped like Olympic swimmers.

Many of the meatheads are not able to complete the required tasks due to their physical makeup. It is not what you look like on the outside, rather it is what you have inside that allows someone to excel in an adverse situation.

I have already spoken of mental toughness, but the mind is a powerful weapon. Mental strength is what separates the good leader from the great leader. Someone born with tons of natural ability and talent with mediocre work ethic may not make it as far as a mentally strong person with average ability. The traits that a bullet-resistant person incorporates into his or her structure are a positive attitude, self-control, and calmness under fire. When you add these traits to a Spirit-filled, biblically rooted foundation, the combination will better prepare you for action when the rounds start coming down range.

No matter what your endeavor is, strap on the full armor of God. Maybe you are a high school athlete or a minister. You could possibly desire to become a special operations warrior, a musician, or even a computer engineer. If you wish to be successful, you must prepare for and be ready to counterattack and defeat the enemy. This is especially important if you wish to stay true to your Christian values. Make sure you realize that we are not born bullet resistant. Our toughness is developed through the strengthening process as we deal with our trials and tribulations in life. Prepare yourself for success. Reach your full potential by putting on the whole armor of God. God's armor is an outstanding defensive element that will protect you in tough times.

EARN YOUR CRACK

"Earn Your Crack" is a phrase that originated in the Marine Corps reconnaissance community. If you look at the unit insignia of 1st Recon Battalion, which is easily the most recognized in the Marine Corps, you will notice that a human skull is centered. On the skull, there is a crack and three bullet holes. Each individually holds their own significance. The crack on the skull is widely understood to represent the trials and hardships that the operator has gone through in preparation for any mission that he is given. The preparation, hard work, sacrifice, and time spent training to perfect the skills of the trade are what will enable the reconnaissance team to succeed. Additionally, the three bullet holes represent the focus and attention to detail that is required to achieve proper sight alignment and sight picture when you must make your hits count. For only through embracing and conquering the hardships of life are we able to acquire the knowledge and ability that is needed for mission success.

Whether you are coaching athletes to perform on the gridiron, preparing warriors for combat, developing a plan for your start-up company's success, or creating a plan and vision for children's Sunday school, you are going to be faced with challenges. Once you accept the challenge, begin to take the first few steps toward your goal, but make sure that you keep your eyes on the objective. You will face challenges. You will have setbacks. How you deal with the adversity that is thrown at you will determine the reputation you make for yourself.

Christian leadership is not a popularity contest. Christian leaders have more at stake, so their actions and reactions matter. Stay focused on growing relationships with those whom you can impact. Empower others, and provide them opportunities to grow. Be genuine and authentic. Show the people who look to you and depend on you that you are willing to take calculated risks to help them further themselves. Invest in others. Understand that your leadership style must be one that does not threaten. Your approach needs to make others feel comfortable. This is important because when the opportunity arises to speak to someone about the Lord, you need to be genuine and have authenticity.

Winning people over is a process in itself that can take time and a tremendous amount of patience. Take advantage of the resources at your disposal. Search out for additional resources and make sure to invest in others. Show people that you are no different than they are, but you have someone who always has your back.

You are going to struggle with day-to-day issues and problems just like everyone else. Make sure you have a *Bible buddy* that you can count on to help or correct your course when times get hard. Invite coworkers, neighbors, and friends to church. Make it clear that by inviting people to church, you are not trying to suck them into a cult. Rather, you just want to be a part of their life. They are free to come to their own conclusions about God's grace. Salvation is an event. Grace allows us to be set free from our sin. It is important to know that just accepting Jesus into your heart and knowing that he unselfishly died on the cross for our sins are not enough.

If I was named the head coach of the Dallas Cowboys, I would be excited. This in itself would be a great event. But once the fanfare died down, I would have to get to work. I would have to learn all of the integral processes and procedures that are associated with the National Football League. I would dive into the rules and policies that apply as well as learn the steps, methods, and practices used to acquire athletes and finally work to develop each of my athletes to their full potential. Only after I have accomplished each of these goals would I have the potential to earn a championship.

Just as I would have to develop and grow my athletes, it is important that we constantly grow our connection to and relationship with Jesus. I cannot state enough the importance of drawing closer to God. It is crucial that we develop a strong personal relationship with God. Our Christian growth has to be a process that never ends. Jesus died on the cross so that we could spend eternity in heaven, but he desires that we do more. I know no other sacrifice that is more powerful.

> Greater love has no one than this: to lay down
> one's life for one's friends. (John 15:13)

Jesus sacrificed for us. It is our duty and responsibility to win people over for him. This, overall, brings honor to Christ.

We are all sinners. We all make mistakes. Every church you enter is full of imperfect people. As Christian leaders, it is important that we never forget that we are no different than the next man. However, it is our actions that depict what we truly stand for. Make it clear that Christianity is not manipulation, rather Christianity is all about integration. As a Christian leader, provide an opportunity for those around you to recognize something that they are missing. Be the spark. Be open and honest, kind and forgiving, patient and considerate.

Finally, if you are a strong witness, you will come upon obstacles and be ambushed by the devil. Do not look at the obstruction as something that you cannot conquer; rather, reevaluate your attack plan, and take another approach. Endure for Christ. Stay the course. Be special, and become a Christian difference maker.

I think it best stated here: "My food," said Jesus, "is to do the will of him who sent me and to finish his work. Don't you have a saying, 'It's still four months until harvest'? I tell you, open your eyes and look at the fields! They are ripe for harvest. Even now the one who reaps draws a wage and harvests a crop for eternal life, so that the sower and the reaper may be glad together" (John 4:34–36).

ABOUT THE AUTHOR

Joseph Welock is a passionate Christian American patriot. His mission is to inspire, equip, and mold the next generation of strong Christian leaders. He is a graduate of the University of Texas at Austin and is currently in his twenty-second year coaching high school football. Joseph Welock is a fifth-generation Marine. As an active-duty Marine, his time was spent in both the infantry and reconnaissance communities.

He is married to Amber Welock, his high school sweetheart. Amber is an amazing wife, mother, attorney, and life partner. Together, they have two wonderful daughters, and he thanks God every day for his blessings.

Joseph places major emphasis on educating his students and athletes on the importance of integrity, dependability, and servant leadership. His coaching, teaching, and writing are rooted in his faith and military background. He believes that we are modern-day "spiritual warriors," and if we truly wish to be victorious, each of us must understand the role and responsibility that we have ahead of us. Joseph hopes that this book will be a valuable resource as you prepare for victory on the battlefield of life.